# THE
# Home Physician

*Compiled by*
## ROLFE COBLEIGH
*Associate Editor of American Agriculturist*

*With the Advice and Assistance of*
## ERDIX T. SMITH, M.D.
*Practicing Physician, and Surgeon to Wesson
Memorial Hospital, Springfield, Mass.*

## BURFORD BOOKS

## PUBLISHER'S NOTE AND DISCLAIMER

*The Home Physician* reflects medical thinking of a century ago and this edition is intended only as an item of historical interest. It is NOT presented, and should not be construed, as legitimate advice on health. In no event will the Publisher be liable for any loss, damage, or injury relating to the use of this book. Any questions on health matters should be directed to a qualified health professional.

First published 1910 by Orange Judd Company.

The special contents of this edition copyright © 2010 by Burford Books, Inc.

Introduction copyright © 2010 by Neal S. Kleiman.

All Rights Reserved. Inquiries should be addressed to: Burford Books, Inc., info@burfordbooks.com.

Printed in the United States of America.

10  9  8  7  6  5  4  3  2  1

Library of Congress Cataloging-in-Publication Data is on file with the Library of Congress.

# Introduction to the 2010 Edition

AS A PRACTICING CARDIOLOGIST, I found myself both intrigued and surprised by *The Home Physician*. Modern medicine is characterized by a fairly close, although somewhat loose relationship with science. Physicians in training spend countless hours learning about what's called 'basic science'—cellular physiology, biochemistry and genetics. Then, as they enter the clinical realm, 'science' takes on a new meaning—application of the scientific method to answer clinical questions and assessment of the evidence that a given treatment works, or doesn't work. The latter approach was really developed only within the past 30 years. During this time, there has been an important shift from recommending treatments that ought to work, to recommending treatments that have been shown to be effective and to improve patients' outcomes. Therefore, one might expect the contents of a century old home medical guide to be replete with superstition and beliefs that have been thoroughly refuted by modern medical science. Recognize, for example, that the germ theory of disease was not fully accepted at that time, no one knew what a virus was, there were no antibiotics, the EKG had only been invented six years previously, and DNA would not be recognized as the medium through which genetic information was transmitted for another forty years. Although Pasteur noted that certain bacteria were able to kill other bacteria, the first antibiotic, salvarsan (the arsenic-based "magic bullet" used to treat syphilis), did not become available until the year following *The Home Physician*'s publication.

It's surprising then, that more than a few statements made in *The Home Physician* haven't changed much in the past century. An introductory paragraph, for example, includes the attestation "There are many things about certain organs that are not yet understood by the wisest men." It is almost certain that the authors had very little clue how much that statement would ring true one hundred years later. Another paragraph contains the statement "A large part of the illness from which we suffer is caused by improper eating." Certainly, no physician alive in 2010, would disagree with this assertion. However, few studies have been performed to inform us of what constitutes "proper" eating, and no two physicians can agree beyond a few basic principles on what constitutes a healthful diet. The authors advise frequent exercise, avoiding tobacco and excessive alcohol consumption, just as most physicians would today, although they are clearly incorrect in classifying these two substances as 'narcotics'. Similarly, the detailed recommendations for preparation of a room for delivery of an infant, are not too far from current standards. There is a good deal of detail given to maintaining cleanliness and making the environment comfortable for the mother, as well as detail concerning the appropriate attire for the delivery nurse. Of course today's standards aren't identical, but the attempt to codify them is a precursor to the detailed standard operating procedures that hospitals are currently required to maintain by various accreditation and regulatory organizations. The latter include strict standards of asepsis and dress codes for the delivery room. Interestingly, the recommendation for window with a southern exposure is reminiscent of many current department of health codes that require an exterior-facing window for each bed in an intensive care unit. Of course, the compendium of medications listed on page 75 is rather comical. Such substances as carbolic acid (phenol), tar, sulphuric acid, and turpentine would be difficult to find on any hospital formulary or insurer's list of preferred medications. Similarly, other recommendations contained in the book reflect predominant social beliefs of its era, such as the belief that masturbation causes insanity. On the other hand, some of the prescribed cures represent what many people feel is lacking in modern medicine — recognition that it is very difficult to effect a change in an individual's medical condition without altering his or her environment. Thus, sections are devoted to elimination of rodents from a house, and to the best way to kill mosquitoes.

As such, the book has a certain charm. Since disease-modifying treatments were few and far between at that time, there are many quaint recommendations that few people would scoff at today. The recommendations for frequent sitz baths and cold foot baths doesn't find much support in the medical literature, but truthfully it is hard to argue with them. Anyone who looks to this book in the twenty-first century as a source of medical information is in serious trouble from the outset. However, for anyone curious to see how medicine has changed over the past century, *The Home Physician* provides an interesting window.

Neal S. Kleiman, MD

# TABLE OF CONTENTS

**RETURN TO NATURE**

Little children delight in nakedness. Aside from the demands of civilization, clothes seem to be necessary in these northern lands to protect the body from cold, but every day, in a warm room, small children should enjoy the invigorating pleasure that comes to them in freedom from their more or less burdensome apparel, and exercise with the air in contact with their bodies.

---

*BLESSED health! thou art above all gold and treasure; 'tis thou who enlargest the soul, and openest all its powers to receive instruction, and to relish virtue. He that hath thee hath little more to wish for! and he that is so wretched as to want thee, wants everything with thee.*
*—[Sterne.*

# INTRODUCTION

HEALTH, happiness and success naturally go together. Because they do, and because each is so dependent upon each other and inseparably combined, when we seek one wisely we seek all. Thus only is life made worth living. There may seem to be a few exceptions, but one cannot fairly challenge the rule that good health is the foundation of achievement. Ever since the printed page came into being, men have been making books and trying to tell men how to deal with the great problem of disease. Thousands of books are upon the market that set forth more or less truthfully, more or less intelligibly, and more or less completely, the facts that relate to the physical health, the nature and treatment of diseases. Wise and consecrated men have devoted their lives through all ages to the study of the various branches of this subject. From the darkness, mystery and error of long ago, constant and, in our time, rapid progress has been made in the discovery of the causes of disease, and the ways and means of most effectively treating it. A treatise on any given disease written a few years ago may be entirely obsolete today. Things which were guessed at a while ago may have since been entirely proved or disproved. Medical writers have never been able to say the final word in the past,

and cannot even today. This means that many of the books that we have been inclined to look upon as authoritative are of little value now, and new books are needed to tell the new facts that the new days have brought us.

We have thought we were performing what is likely to prove to be a real public service in compiling The Home Physician. Next to the Bible there is no book that any of us needs so much as a reliable book telling us what we ought to know about the care of our bodies. At the time The Home Physician is written, there is no other book of like moderate size which contains so much reliable information about the nature and treatment of diseases and the proper care of the body as does this volume. It is not intended to take the place of the good family doctor, but to supplement his services, and to help our friends to take better care of themselves and their families, to the end that they may be happier, more efficient, better in every sense, and may live longer in the world. We do not intend to exhaust the subjects treated nor to tell all that is worth telling and knowing about them. Of course, we could not do so. We have tried to gather together and present in language that all can understand just as many of the most important things as the space of one book of convenient size will hold. Special care has been taken to exclude doubtful theories and to include well-proven facts. We have tried to bring our information up to date, in several instances including discoveries that have been made within a year.

## THE GUESSWORK OF DOCTORING

The practice of medicine cannot be termed an exact science. Men have not yet been able to formulate and attach fixed and invariable rules with reference to the functions and diseases of the various parts of the body. There are many things about certain organs that are not yet understood by the wisest men. Then there is another fact always to be remembered, that there is a great difference in people. The difference may be broadly described as a difference of temperament. A certain disease manifests itself differently in different persons and certain medicines have often exactly opposite effects on different persons.

Then, in the matter of drugs and other remedies used in the treatment of diseases, there is much yet to be learned. One of the very good reasons why those of us who are not physicians should not meddle with most drugs without expert advice is that even the best educated experts do not know all about most of those drugs themselves, and serious, often fatal, results follow not only an overdose of a certain preparation, but its use at all under certain conditions.

One of the warnings which cannot be too often repeated nor too greatly emphasized is not to use drugs without the advice of a physician, unless you are absolutely certain that no harm can result from the particular drug in question when used for the particular purpose receiving attention. And with this should always go another warning: Do not delay sending for a physician when symptoms of disease are manifested which may indicate something serious. Many ailments, treated promptly as they should be, do not prove at all serious, but delay in such treatment may be a matter of life and death.

## Caution and Precaution

There are certain standard drugs that may be depended upon for certain purposes which every family should always keep on hand. But it is a pretty good rule to avoid the use of drugs, except when prescribed by a physician, and to use instead simple home remedies that are not drugs. It ought to make one pretty serious and thoughtful in this matter of treating diseases when we reflect that a very large part of all the doctoring is a matter of guesswork. If the guess is wrong, the patient— or victim, perhaps, he should be called—may die. This is one of the many reasons why the ounce of prevention should always be considered before the pound of cure.

We would not disparage for a moment the wonderful achievements of men of science in the great fields of medicine and modern surgery. The achievements of these men to a remarkable degree have lengthened life, eased suffering, and added immeasurably to the happiness and powers of mankind. In these days it is truer than ever before when we say, " While there is life there is hope." The list of so-called incurable diseases is steadily growing less. There are only a very few now which cannot be successfully treated, if treated properly in their earliest stages.

# How to Avoid Sickness

THERE is no more appalling fact in this world than the great waste that attends human life and things that man does and endures. If the life of every man and woman could be at least three score years and ten, and during that span every man and woman could be well, how mightily would be multiplied the possibilities of achievement, of material production, of mental, moral and physical progress! The average life is one-half cut off by disease and the half that remains is half wasted by bodily ailments. A large part of all this waste and the attendant suffering and sorrow is preventable by the use of a little knowledge of fundamental principles of right living and the exercising of plain common sense.

Civilized people do not live correctly. Savages do not live correctly. Each has certain advantages over the other in certain particulars. A happy medium lies between, where, combining the wisdom of both, we may live long and well. Efficiency and happiness in this world depend so largely upon good health, that it is well worth while to make a serious study of the problem how to avoid sickness and what to do when sick. As an ounce of prevention is always worth a pound of cure, what we ought to know first is how to avoid sickness.

11

## RULES OF HEALTH

The fundamental rules of health are simple, but it is not always easy to live the simple life and at the same time live as vigorously as the times require. But it pays. Be sure of this: Most sickness is avoidable. Most people who call themselves well can greatly increase their powers of body and mind by taking better care of themselves. By the way, it is worth remembering that the powers of mind are largely dependent on the good health of the body, and the converse of this, which is equally true, is that the condition of the body is largely controlled by the mind. Every one of the established rules of health is simply an application of common sense to the care of the body.

Whatever you do, don't waste your money and make a bad matter worse by pouring patent medicines through your system, unless such medicines have been prescribed by a physician or you really know that they will do you good and not harm. And never, never use stuff advertised as cures for serious diseases by men whom you do not know. At least 99 per cent of such things are the wickedest of frauds.

Here are some of the simple rules of health. Each is easy to follow; each sounds commonplace; each, however, is of vital importance, and together they insure good health, usually:

### Good Air, Sunshine and Sleep

Breathe good air, and cultivate the habit of breathing deeply so as to get plenty of air and keep all parts of the lungs healthy by constant exercise. Take special care to have plenty of fresh air during sleeping hours. No one can enjoy perfect health or have sound, refreshing sleep unless the bedroom windows are opened part way at least. Fear of night air is a fallacy.

Sunshine is one of the important things to seek, and the sun is one of the most potent enemies of disease and disease germs that exists. The best air to breathe is that which has recently received the rays of the sun, as the rays of the sun have a health-giving effect upon the human body. Every living room should receive the rays of the sun for a time during every twenty-four hours.

Sleep enough of the twenty-four hours to secure the rest and refreshment you need. Different persons require different time for sleep, some more, some less. An adult should have an average of at least seven hours, some require eight, and others find six sufficient, but children require more, and they should take as much as they can get. The old rule of " Early to bed and early to rise " is a good one. In the matter of sleep, as in the matter of all other things, regularity and a definite time for doing this is important. The organs of the body perform their functions with less likelihood of disorder if regular habits are formed and maintained.

### Bathing Benefits

Inasmuch as cleanliness is essential to health, regular and thorough bathing should be one of the daily habits of life. A hot bath tends to be debilitating and a very cold bath may so shock a weak body that its effect may be injurious. To those who can stand it, a cold bath in the morning, quickly taken—and there are few who cannot stand a quickly taken cold bath—is very invigorating. The time to take a hot bath is at night. Absolute cleanliness is the one important thing to consider.

## Eating to Live

A large part of the illness from which we suffer is caused by improper eating. Eating should be at regular intervals and the food should be chewed until completely reduced to liquid form, which cannot be done in a hurry. Many cases of dyspepsia are caused by hurried eating and improper mastication.

The diet should be limited to plain, nutritious food of good quality and properly cooked, if cooked at all. Green and overripe fruit should be avoided, and animal foods that have begun to spoil should never be eaten. A mixed diet is the best. It is not only pleasanter to eat a variety of foods from day to day, but the best chemical elements needed for nourishment are best obtained through variety. There is much to be said for the vegetarian diet, but for most people it proves unsatisfactory in the long run, and the natural thing is for some meat to be made a part of each day's food. Most Americans err in the direction of eating too much meat.

In order that eating may be most beneficial, there should be a brief period of relaxation before each meal and a similar period afterward. A great aid to digestion is good nature, and one should cultivate the habit of cheerfulness and laughter during meals. If there is any scolding to be done, save it for some other time. Always stop eating while you feel that you could eat more.

## Keep the Bowels Regular

It is of great importance that the bowels should be kept regular and in a healthy condition. If there is a tendency to constipation matters are made worse in the long run by the taking of medicines. It is best to cure the trouble by changing the diet, eating more fruit and vegetables, as those foods are for a laxative effect. Drink plenty of water, especially between meals, just after rising in the morning and just before retiring at night. If most of us would drink twice as much as we do we would be better off; but we should not wash down our food with water or with any other drinks. Good water is the best drink, and the less tea, coffee or other drinks of a stimulating nature that we indulge in the better.

A tendency to constipation is often relieved by the practice of exercises which call into play the muscles of the abdomen. Walking does this to a certain extent. The abdominal muscles may be exercised more effectively by raising and lowering the legs one at a time, and together, while in a reclining position. If the abdominal muscles are kept healthy by exercise there is rarely ever any trouble from constipation. A further aid is establishing a regular habit of going to the stool at the same time every day and always responding promptly to the calls of nature.

## Daily Exercise Necessary

Exercise is one of the necessities attendant upon health. Some persons require more than others, but all require daily exercise, a liberal part of which should be in the open air. Exercise should be taken vigorously, but not to the extent of strain or over-exertion. Daily exercise should bring into play all the muscles of the body.

A fairly long walk should be part of the daily

exercise, and while walking one should cultivate the habit of erect and graceful carriage, breathing deeply of the pure air that has been vitalized by sunshine. Don't omit your daily walk because of bad weather, but dress so as to properly protect yourself from the elements.

## Health in Dress

Proper dress is another element in maintaining good health. Adapt the clothing to weather conditions as well as possible. Protect the body from exposure to the cold, but avoid the mistake that many make of wearing too heavy clothing. This is largely a matter of habit. One object to be sought is the so-called hardening of the body. This is secured by cold baths and light clothing. A person accustomed to wearing light clothing in cold weather is much less likely to take cold than one who always bundles up. The throat and chest should not be overprotected.

The feet should always be well protected from cold and dampness. Those who are not in good vigor should always be careful to avoid a serious chill and should not be led into discomfort by any fanatical ideas about wearing less clothing than they really need.

## Success Through Self-Control

An important habit to cultivate is that of periods of repose. This is especially needed by persons of nervous temperament. Only as we are masters of ourselves and have self-control, are we able to do our own best work, and to effectively influence others. Self-control cannot be secured without daily periods of calm near the middle of the day. It is a good plan to have a quiet period of a half hour, when we may sit alone and dismiss all care and worry from the mind. We gain needed reserve power by mental and physical relaxation.

The mind has a great power over the body. It makes all the difference between sickness and health whether we cultivate the right habits of mind. If really sick, one is made worse by worry and fret, and better by cheerfulness, confidence and hope. Many persons believe themselves sick and many are invalids because they think they have troubles which exist only in the mind. Disagreeable states of mind are produced by worry, anger, hatred and jealousy, which often impair the health. Pleasant states of mind are produced by hope, confidence, cheerfulness and love. Will power is improved by positive habits of thinking. They make not only more healthy men, but more effective and successful workers, either of brain or hand.

## Keep on Playing

The best health and the fine art of keeping young require the habitual cultivation of the play spirit. Play is a universal characteristic of childhood. We are all children—of older growth, perhaps, but children none the less if we are in good health. Never allow yourself to get out of sympathy with child life and the pleasures of children. Refuse to grow old. Keep the child spirit in your life—that is, the spirit of play. Have some fun every day of your life. Never quit playing. Wholesome games involving more or less physical exercise keep people young and help mightily to keep them in good health.

## CARE OF THE TEETH

Sound, well-kept teeth not only contribute to good looks but to good health. Civilized man can hardly expect to have good teeth unless he takes special pains to keep them clean and in good repair. If particles of food are permitted to remain between the teeth they decompose and the acids and gases thus formed soon dissolve the enamel of the teeth and start the process of decay. Once begun, the process goes steadily forward. A cavity in the teeth is a breeding place for germs, which not only ruin the teeth, but create an unhealthy state of affairs, making the breath offensive and often causing stomach trouble.

The teeth should be carefully cleaned after each meal, and before going to bed special care should be taken to brush the teeth thoroughly, so that nothing may remain in contact with them that will tend toward decay during the night. Brushing should be up and down, rather than simply across the teeth. If one would be thorough about it, teeth may be kept clean with the use of only clear water, a good tooth brush and a little muscle. Many feel the need of tooth powder, however.

There are good tooth powders upon the market, but they are more expensive than the powders which we may prepare at home, and no more effective. Some tooth powders contain powerful acids which will remove stains and whiten the teeth, but injure the enamel, and, therefore, should be avoided.

### A Good Tooth Powder

A harmless and effective tooth powder may be made of four parts, by weight, precipitated chalk, one part orris root, one part powdered castile soap, well mixed, to which may be added a few drops of oil of wintergreen. A good tooth wash is a solution of common salt and water. Among the best antiseptic washes is diluted dioxygen. Frequent use of an antiseptic wash is advisable. A tooth brush should be at least of moderate stiffness, in order to do its work well, but it should not be harsh enough to injure the gums.

The teeth should be inspected at least twice a year by a dentist, and as soon as a cavity is discovered it should be filled. At least twice a year teeth should be cleaned by a dentist, who removes the accumulated deposit of tartar that it is practically impossible to remove with a brush, especially on the back teeth.

It is no longer considered in good taste to display a lot of gold in the mouth. So far as conditions warrant, the filling of front teeth by the best dentists now is accomplished largely with porcelain, which closely resembles the color of the teeth, and is very durable.

## CARE OF THE HAIR

Most people, especially men, find it difficult to keep the hair in good condition. Indeed, it is not always possible to keep it at all. The hair itself should be kept clean and the scalp should be kept clean, but the use of soap should be limited to the actual necessities of cleanliness. Strong soap should never be used. Metal combs and metal hair brushes should not be used, as they tend to injure both the hair and the scalp. Daily brushing with a good clean bristle brush helps to keep the hair healthy, clean and strong, as well as to encourage its growth. Thorough but careful massage of the scalp with the finger tips, avoiding any scratching with the nails, is beneficial. Nearly all hair dye is dangerous and should never be used. Most so-called hair tonics are fraudulent.

## Hair Tonics

One of the best hair tonics is common kerosene oil, which should be applied once a month, a drop in a place, upon the scalp with a medicine dropper, or better still, a small bicycle or sewing machine oiler. It stops falling hair and promotes a more vigorous growth. Strong sage tea as a daily wash will often stop the hair from falling out, and its use persisted in may cause the hair to grow thick and strong.

Baldness is caused by disease germs which attack the hair roots. The only way to stop falling hair is to kill these germs. This is partially accomplished by free exposure to the air and sunshine. The remedies suggested above have the effect of destroying germs. They also help to keep the scalp healthy.

## NARCOTIC HABITS

### Tobacco

Tobacco is a narcotic, owing to the presence of a poisonous alkaloid called nicotine. During the process of smoking or chewing tobacco, a variable amount of this poison is absorbed into the system. If an overdose is taken, as often occurs with beginners, a sudden dizziness is produced, with weakness, pallor, and cold, clammy sweat, and intense nausea, followed by vomiting and purging. The

effect of long-continued and excessive use of tobacco varies in different individuals. It may appear
as an irritation of the throat and upper air passages,
due to the action of the heated vapor.

In pipe smokers the effect is more often upon the
lips and tongue, making those organs more liable
to cancerous disease. Dyspepsia and loss of flesh
frequently result from swallowing the saliva containing nicotine. Palpitation and irregular action
of the heart, and nervous conditions commonly result from its absorption, while a serious impairment
of vision sometimes occurs.

## A Habit Hard to Break

The bad effects of tobacco usually disappear soon
after discontinuing the drug, but the tobacco habit,
like other drug habits, is difficult to break off, and
its sudden withdrawal sometimes causes grave
symptoms. The cigarette habit appears to be especially hard to discontinue, and those who are addicted to it seem to require its almost constant use.
The abnormal quantity smoked, and the fact that
cigarette smoke is almost invariably inhaled, makes
this form of smoking particularly objectionable.

Cigars contain much more nicotine than cigar-
ettes. Men engaged in active muscular exercise
suffer less from the use of tobacco than those leading sedentary lives, and adults less than youths.
A pipe smoked for a short time, following the evening meal, by those who have performed a hard day's
work, aids digestion, soothes the overwrought
nerves and induces repose.

## Alcohol

Alcohol is a narcotic poison. In various forms it
has its value in medicine and chemistry. The best

rule is to take alcoholic liquors into the system only when it is needed for medicinal purposes and to avoid its use in any form or quantity habitually. Like tobacco, it is especially harmful to the young. Its primary effect upon the body is to cause partial paralysis of certain nerves which control the blood vessels. This paralysis causes the blood vessels in the skin to dilate. The blood rushes to the surface, producing a feeling of warmth, while at the same time the interior of the body becomes cooler and the vitality is lowered, and the power of the body lessened.

This nerve paralysis caused by alcohol is more extensive in habitual indulgence, and the system becomes an easy prey to bacterial infection and less capable of withstanding such disease attacks, while the continual use of alcohol, even by the so-called moderate drinker, produces a slow poisoning of the vital organs, heart, kidneys, liver or brain, which results in a serious disease of one or more of these organs. The mucous membranes of the stomach and other digestive organs also become more or less inflamed.

## SOURCES OF CONTAGION

There are so many ways in which contagious diseases are spread that it is difficult to anticipate and protect one's self against them all. Indeed, this is practically impossible. There are, however, several sources of contagion against which one should be constantly on the guard. One of these is the general sanitary conditions of the home. This includes cleanliness inside of the house, thorough screening in summer to keep out insects, the use of disinfectants when needed in the drains or elsewhere, proper drainage and an absolutely pure source of water supply free from any danger of contamination through drainage, either on the surface or underground.

Well water should never be used for drinking unless the well is so located that it is impossible for it to be contaminated by underground drainage from any source of filth. Some diseases, notably typhoid fever, are usually spread through water. If possible, the house should stand a little higher than the other farm buildings and far enough from the barns and outbuildings where flies breed in great numbers, that swarms of flies will not be dividing their time between the house and the filth from which they come.

### Beware of Insects

The common house fly has been proved to be a serious source of contagion and spreads disease germs and filth wherever it goes. Food should be kept well screened and doors and windows of the house well screened against flies. The screening should be thorough enough to keep out mosquitos also, for they are another source of contagion. One variety makes a business of spreading malaria by carrying the germ from a person who has the disease, and inserting it with his lancelike bill into a healthy person. Another variety of mosquito has the spreading of yellow fever for its specialty.

Sluggish ponds and pools of water and swampy places are where mosquitos breed. It is, therefore, important to avoid having such places near dwellings so far as possible. All sluggish water should be removed, by thorough drainage. Damp, low-lying sections should be avoided in selecting a home.

Mosquitos may be destroyed in large numbers, as they begin their career at the breeding places, by pouring coal oil (kerosene) upon the surface of the stagnant water.

## Rats, Mice and Pets

Rats and mice carry diseases, especially rats. Many epidemics of bubonic plague of the Orient, as well as other dangerous diseases, have been caused by rats. There should be no cessation in the efforts to keep the house as free from rats and mice as possible. There is more or less objection to the ordinary methods of poisoning rats, because they are likely to die in the partitions of the house, thus causing added insanitary conditions. Some of the methods commended for driving them away are the following:

Scatter moth balls around the haunts and in the holes through which the rats pass. Dried pieces of sponge dipped in honey and sprinkled with oil of rhodium, scattered in a similar manner, may be recommended. Cayenne pepper sprinkled in rat holes is effective. A thin coating of caustic potash spread in and near the rat holes drives them away. In addition to the common rat traps, rats may be caught by taking a large, deep vessel filled to within six inches of the top with water and the remaining space with bran. Large numbers are sometimes drowned thus.

Cover a barrel half filled with water with stout paper, tying the edges around the barrel. Place food as a bait on top and lean a board against the barrel on one side for the rats to climb up on. Cut a cross in the paper near the center between the board and the bait. The rat falls through this, and

## What Cats Are For

There is just one good reason for keeping a cat. That reason is to kill and drive away rats and mice. Few people realize the great danger to which their children are exposed in playing with cats, however cute and interesting the cat may be. Many contagious diseases are spread in this way.

Seek Health Among the Flowers

the paper returns to place. Often many rats share the same fate and drown in the barrel.

A good cat is usually a reliable rat catcher. A ferret will clean out a building infested with rats. It will also kill chickens and small pets, so it is important to guard against injury to the latter and as soon as the rats have been killed or driven away, the ferret should be removed.

A source of contagion usually not considered but often the cause of serious trouble are pets. Cats and dogs, especially cats, spread many diseases. These animals should be kept clean and, so far as possible, their wanderings should be restricted. It is wisest not to keep pets in the house. The fondling of cats by children should be discouraged.

## Shun the Public Drinking Cup

One of the most serious menaces to public health is the public drinking cup. There is no means by which consumption, for instance, is so surely communicated. Never drink from a cup that others drink from on a train, at a railroad station, or elsewhere. If it seems to be necessary to do so, place the lips within the cup instead of on the edge. It is a good plan whenever one travels to carry a drinking cup or otherwise get along some way without drinking. Paper cups are now made which are very inexpensive. They are carried by travelers and thrown away after being used. Very good collapsible cups can be bought which last for many years, and these may be carried in the pocket. They are handy to carry when on long drives or walks, or for picnics.

A good cup may be made from a piece of strong, clean paper about 9 inches square. Fold it once into a triangular shape. With the long, folded side toward you, fold each lower corner so as to just reach the center of the side opposite that corner, with the farther edges, after folding, just in line over each other. Separate the open right angular corners, and fold one over the side where the other folds are and as far down as it will go, and the other corner to match on the plain side. This forms a cup that will be waterproof for one drink and usually more. If oiled or paraffin paper is used the cup will be much more durable. This is an excellent scheme for travel or picnics.

Inasmuch as children are more susceptible to many diseases than adults, it is best that they should be kept out of crowds.

## DISINFECTANTS AND FUMIGATION

Disinfectants are necessary to protect against and to prevent the spread of diseases. The purpose is to kill the disease germs. These germs are of two kinds, the vegetable, or bacterial, and the animal or parasitic. Some disinfectants are effective in killing one class of germs, but ineffective with another; but certain disinfectants are powerful enough to kill almost any germ if used in sufficient quantity and under proper conditions. Corrosive sublimate is an effective germ killer, and may be used in a solution of one part to five hundred parts water. Infected clothing soaked in this solution before washing, and woodwork wiped with it, will be free from germs. It is very poisonous and should not be taken internally.

Chloride of lime in strong solution is effective as a disinfectant and is used chiefly to cleanse drains. It injures metals and cloths, and so is to be used with care. Clothing may be disinfected by boiling steadily for an hour in water. A great aid to purifying bedding and clothing is sunlight and fresh air. Bad odors may be removed by placing well-ground coffee upon a moderately hot iron plate or roaster and placing it in the room or carrying it about.

## How to Fumigate

Disinfecting by fumigation is accomplished by the use of various substances. One of the most common is sulphur. The sulphur may be put into an iron kettle placed in a pail or pan and enough water poured into the outer vessel to reach half way up the sides of the kettle containing the sulphur. Then the sulphur should be burned, either by pouring in a small quantity of alcohol and setting it on fire, or dropping a few live coals into the sulphur. A part of the water in the outer vessel will be turned into vapor by the heat of the burning sulphur, and this aids in killing the germs. The water is also a protection against fire.

Clothing that would be damaged by sulphur fumes should be removed. Metal surfaces should also be protected by a light coating of vaseline. The room disinfected should be closed six or eight hours, and then thoroughly ventilated.

One of the best disinfectants for fumigation is formalin. To find out the quantity needed, measure the room to be fumigated and multiply the length, breadth and hight together in feet. This will give the number of cubic feet. For each 1,000 cubic feet take one pint of formalin and one pound of fresh lime. This proportion is necessary to produce the right chemical results. The lime may be placed in a tin or earthen dish and the formalin should be poured upon it. This causes the lime to slake and a poisonous gas to be immediately released. The gas kills the germs in the room. Leave the room as soon as possible. Before attempting to fumigate, paper should be pasted over all the cracks, so that the room may be as nearly air proof as possible.

## INSECT PESTS

There are numerous insects, commonly called vermin, whose presence in a house is insanitary and very undesirable. It is often a serious problem how to get rid of them. They sometimes may be killed by fumigation. Fumigation is the surest method of getting rid of fleas, using either sulphur or formalin.

### Ants

These little pests dislike oil of pennyroyal. Pour this oil on bits of cotton batting and spread about the places where the ants appear. If fresh pennyroyal can be procured, spread the leaves about the infested places. Oil of peppermint may also drive away ants.

### Cockroaches

Garbage left standing is one of the surest means of attracting cockroaches. Dissolve one pound of alum in three pints hot water and force a hot solution into all cracks and openings where the roaches are likely to be. Afterward spread borax about the places where the roaches have been in the habit of coming.

Another way is to blow insect powder into all cracks. Brush up and burn the dead insects and powder, and blow in a second dose. Brush up as before and spread powdered borax about the cracks and holes.

## Water Bugs

A weak solution of turpentine poured into the water pipes once a week for a few weeks will usually drive away water bugs. Use one-half pint turpentine to three pints of water. This will drive the bugs from their hiding places and they should then be killed whenever seen. Preparations effective in exterminating cockroaches will usually destroy water bugs.

## Bedbugs

Naphtha is a quick, clean and sure exterminator of this pest. Open all the windows in the room and shake and examine minutely all the bedding. Hang out sheets, blankets, etc.; saturate mattresses, pillows, etc., with naphtha and put them out of doors if possible. Brush the walls of the room, paying special attention to every crack, groove and corner. Examine the backs of all framed pictures. These pests will often hide in the cracks in a picture frame. If there are any ribbons used for decorative purposes, such as hanging photographs, examine the knots closely.

Take up the carpet, take the bedstead apart and lay on the floor with the grooved sides up; saturate with naphtha. Fill with naphtha any cracks or breaks in the walls or floor, then leave the room and lock the door, allowing no one to enter it. If much naphtha is used it is safer to keep the door shut and the windows open for the greater part of the day. Remember that *no fire* must be allowed anywhere near naphtha.

The first application will kill all the living insects, but not the eggs. In three or four days repeat the operation and this will destroy all the bugs which have hatched since the first killing.

## Moths and Buffalo Bugs

The above treatment is equally good for these pests. Of course, the eggs will not be destroyed, and these are gotten rid of by brushing and shaking before the naphtha is applied. Washing out closets spring and fall with a weak solution of carbolic acid is an excellent means of keeping them free from insects.

# SIMPLE HOME REMEDIES

**M**OST people have so firmly established the habit of seeking for things beyond their reach and trying to accomplish things by difficult and expensive means, that they neglect to use simple and cheap things that are right at hand, with which to accomplish the same purposes. It seems to be the weakness of human nature, certainly the human nature of many people, to like to take medicine. They find frequent excuse for the use of strong, dark-colored concoctions that they really don't know anything about, but which somebody tells them are good for what ails them, or for what might be the matter if they needed doctoring at all. The experimental and habitual use of drugs in the form of patent medicines and otherwise without the advice of a physician is one of the dangerous and harmful practices of thousands of people who otherwise exercise common sense in the affairs of life.

It is a pleasant and interesting discovery for most of us to find out how successfully we can get along without drugs, and how many disorders can be successfully treated with common, simple things that are likely to be found in every household. One of the bad things about drugs is that most of them are likely to have a harmful effect if they do not have a beneficial one. Many of the simple home remedies do no harm if they do no good. That is a very important consideration.

## SALT

One of the most familiar substances in every household is common salt. The medicinal uses of salt are many and varied. For example, one of the most stimulating preparations for the bath is a solution of salt and water. The eyes may be strengthened by bathing with a salt solution. It is also good for some forms of sore throat, and is a good mouth wash for the teeth. It may be used as a spray or flushed into the nasal passages to relieve catarrh. Although painful, if too strong, it is effective as a disinfectant for sores or wounds. Salt is an emetic in case of poisoning. For this purpose it should be given freely in warm water.

In a salt water bath the salt does not enter the body, but stimulates the skin, which tends to improve the circulation of the blood and is helpful in cases of general debility, eczema, scrofula and other conditions of blood disorder. A strong salt solution is an effective enema. Solutions of salt are often injected into the veins to increase the amount of fluid in the body following severe bleeding or any surgical shock when the blood pressure is dangerously low. No one other than a skilled physician should attempt to do it, however.

## PEPPER

Pepper comes upon the table as a companion to salt. It also has useful medicinal qualities. It is given in the form of an infusion to induce perspiration and to break up a cold. It is given in certain forms of dyspepsia with some simple bitter. If not too strong its irritating qualities have a stimulating effect upon the membranes of the digestive organs. It is sometimes used externally as a counter irritant to relieve internal inflammation.

## COOKING SODA

Soda of the kind used in cooking, which is called by the chemists bicarbonate of soda, is an excellent remedy for some stomach troubles. It is given to counteract an excess of acid in the stomach and relieves gaseous conditions. It is used as a gargle for sore throat. Soda is one of the best applications for burns, scalds and bites of insects. Solutions of soda are often beneficial when taken for rheumatism, diabetes and gravel in the acid form. There is danger in taking this habitually and in large doses.

## CREAM OF TARTAR

Cream of tartar is known as a laxative in small doses, usually combined with sulphur or magnesia. It is an excellent cathartic. Dissolved in lemonade it often has a beneficial effect upon the kidneys and bladder by increasing the secretion of urine. In large doses it is poisonous.

## MUSTARD

Mustard is used medicinally most often in the form of poultices. These are prepared by taking equal parts of flour and mustard and thoroughly mixing them in warm water to form a paste of easily handled consistency. This is wrapped in clean, thin linen or cotton cloth and applied to the skin. If young children, the proportion of flour should be greater than that of mustard, and, in all cases, the poultice should be removed as soon as painful sensations are felt, to prevent blistering. A thorough reddening of the skin is always desired. It has the effect of stimulating the nervous system. Almost all forms of local pain may be removed at least partially by the application of a mustard poultice.

Its use is recommended for rheumatism, neuralgia, toothache, gout, vomiting, diarrhea and in the treatment of bronchitis, pleurisy and pneumonia. Mustard has a tendency to induce sleep, and mustard baths are beneficial in relieving hysteria and convulsions, and in the form of foot baths in relieving headaches and various internal congestions. Mustard and water is used internally as an emetic in cases of poisoning. Mild solutions of mustard sometimes stop hiccough. It also relieves some forms of dyspepsia attended by constipation and is useful to promote digestion and keep the bowels regular.

## GINGER

Ginger acts as a stimulant when taken internally, and relieves colic, certain forms of diarrhea and dyspepsia. It is also used externally for the relief of muscular rheumatism, neuralgia, toothache and headache, being applied either in the form of a poultice or a liquid preparation in which cloths are dipped and thereby applied. Tincture of ginger is considered more effective for internal use than powdered ginger mixed with hot water, but the effects are practically the same. The dose is one teaspoonful, well diluted.

## WATER

We are not inclined to think of water as having any special medicinal value, unless it is one of the so-called mineral waters or contains some medical substance in solution. Pure water may be used in many ways so as to give benefits as positive as a medicine. Most people do not drink water enough, especially between meals. One should not drink to the point of discomfort, of course, but frequent drinks cleanse and flush out the system, preventing many troubles of the kidneys and digestive organs. Dyspepsia is often thus relieved, also bowel troubles. One of the best treatments for chronic constipation is taking a liberal drink of water the first thing upon rising in the morning and a similar drink the last thing before retiring.

Many spells of sickness from indigestion, with attendant headaches and discomfort of the digestive organs, can be prevented by refraining from the use of any food at the time the next meal would naturally be taken, or better still, for the full 24 hours, following the first symptoms of indigestion, drinking freely and frequently pure water. Some people find the treatment more effective, or at least more to their liking, by taking hot water. Sometimes, when a cold appears to be coming on, it may be broken up by drinking all the hot water one comfortably can just before retiring. Of course, this encourages perspiration as well as internal flushing. Sluggish conditions of the bowels are often corrected and the general health thereby immediately improved by enemas of warm water.

There is an endless variety of baths, taken in an endless variety of ways for the relief of an endless variety of diseases. It is safe enough to say that most people bathe altogether too little. One of the most positively beneficial means of stimulating the entire system is a quick, cold bath taken soon after rising in the morning, followed by a brisk rub.

## SOAP

Pure olive oil soap has its use for many more purposes simply than that of cleansing. Soap suds are effective as an enema. Soap suppositories are used to move the bowels of young children. Liniment made from soap is good for the treatment of sprains and bruises. It is also the basis of other liniments. Soap is used internally as an antidote for acid poisoning.

## LEMON JUICE

Lemon juice is one of the most agreeable and at the same time one of the most valuable home remedies for certain purposes. It is effective in the treatment of torpid conditions of the liver and jaundice. It has a beneficial effect in some cases of rheumatism, and has a stimulating effect on the kidneys and bladder. It is a most effective remedy for the prevention and cure of scurvy. Hot lemonade is taken to break up colds.

## HONEY

Bees' honey, drained from the comb, has a stimulating effect on the mucous membranes. It is used for thrush and ulcers of the mouth; and in a mixture of powdered borax and glycerin, being painted upon the sore spots. The mixture is two parts borax, one part glycerin and 16 parts honey.

## WHITE OF EGG

This egg albumen diluted with water is a valuable article of food in the diarrheal complaints of children. It is a convenient and effective antidote in poisoning by corrosive sublimate and sulphate of copper. It forms insoluble compounds with them. Mixed with a little powdered alum it thickens and forms a convenient and soothing poultice for burns, bruises, and bites and stings of insects.

## OLIVE OIL

In addition to being a popular article of diet, olive oil is one of the best mild laxatives for young children. Used habitually it has the effect of toning up the system generally, not only as a food tonic, but by stimulating the digestive activity. It is supposed to increase the flow of bile. Children suffering from poor nutrition may be benefited by rubbing olive oil into the skin, and applied externally it relieves the pain and swelling caused by insect bites and stings. It is also used for burns in the eye. It should not be used in the ear or upon the open wounds, as it forms a breeding material for bacteria.

In the department of medicines will be found reference to many articles which might properly be classed among the Simple Home Remedies. Their use should be encouraged in preference to drugs that are more or less dangerous, and at the same time are often quite expensive.

## LIME WATER

This may be purchased at a drug store or made at home. The formula is one pound of fresh lime

dissolved in eight quarts of distilled water. The
lime should first be slaked with a little water, and
then the remaining water should be added and
well stirred. The solution should set in a covered
vessel three hours. It may then be kept in closed
glass bottles, drawing off the clear portion for use.
It is given in food mixtures to correct acid conditions of the digestive organs of young children.
It sometimes relieves nausea. It may be applied
locally for the relief of eczema and ulcers.

> Joy, temperance and repose,
> Slam the door on the doctor's nose.
> —[Longfellow.

> We seem ambitious God's whole work to undo;
> With new diseases on ourselves we war,
> And with new physic, a worse engine far.
> —[Donne.

# CURES (without) DRUGS

E are coming more and more to realize that most of the ills to which the flesh is heir can be cured without drugs. Physicians and laymen who have made a study of the matter know that the use of drugs in treating diseases is largely experimental; that, to a very large degree, as drugs are indiscriminately used, they do more harm than good. Many people, whose heads are filled with the exaggerated, misleading and often entirely false claims made in the advertisements of patent medicines, seek relief for every ache and pain or imaginary ailment in some preparation which they innocently believe will help them, or at least will do no harm, if it does no good. The fact is that all patent medicines are more or less fraudulent. They do not, and cannot, cure the diseases they are advertised to cure.

Worse than this, it is a fact that harmful narcotics and other dangerous drugs are freely used in preparation of many patent medicines, so that their use is actually dangerous. The national pure food law and the pure food laws of many of the states are intended to regulate this sort of thing, and to prevent the sale of certain especially dangerous drugs, except in very small quantities, in proprietary medicines. These laws have made conditions better than they formerly were, but have come far short of stopping the evil. The liquor habit and the worst drug habits are frequently formed by taking unsuspectingly these things in patent medicines.

It is quite natural that people of moderate means, as well as the poor, should seek to save money by dosing themselves instead of paying a doctor to dose them. Oftentimes this is not economical, because they are unable to select the proper treatment and much valuable time is wasted, during which the disease may progress to an incurable stage. There are certain acute diseases that may be cured by the proper use of certain drugs. There are certain remedies that should be kept on hand for use in emergencies, but the use of drugs should be limited to such cases as seem to actually require drug treatment.

To those who have been accustomed to take drugs freely upon the slightest excuse, or occasionally upon general principles, it is surprising to learn how securely health may be safeguarded and how frequently various disorders may be cured without the use of drugs.

## The Ounce That Is Worth Tons

Under this subject consideration should first be given naturally to the observance of the general and special rules of health which may be dictated by ordinary common sense and which are set forth in some detail in the chapter How to Avoid Sickness, and other parts of this book. If the observance of all the fundamental rules of health is established in the daily habits of our life, most people will be kept in so nearly perfect health and in such vigor of mind and body that the common run of diseases is avoided, and, when disease does come, the body is in shape to throw it off and make a good recovery more quickly and effectively than would otherwise be the case. An ounce of prevention in matters of health is worth tons of cure. The same habits that prevent disease contribute to its cure.

## Mind Power in Health

In all affairs of life there is danger in extremes. Success is found in the happy medium, except in matters of absolute right and wrong. The extremist blazes the way for reform, and whatever he proves to be good should be made use of after its value has been proved. Most of us have not been able to adopt the radical ideas of extremists who believe that the mind is so all powerful that every disease can be cured by the mind, and that drugs should never be used. However, the will to be well, the will to achieve, the will to excel, attended by consistent common sense, hygienic habits and consecration to the high ideals of service almost certainly assure health, happiness and the most complete success in life.

We cannot afford to forget the old maxim: " As a man thinketh so is he." Brooding over troubles, worrying about one's self when one happens to have an off day, thinking about and talking about the symptoms of disease—worry of any kind— make people sick. Such is the power of the mind over the body.

## Science Proves It

Science has only just begun to learn of the wonderful powers of the mind. Hypnotism, telepathy and suggestion are some of the mysterious mind powers that science has proved to be real. Not only can a person help himself to become well and to keep well by his powers of mind, but he can help others in a similar manner through the exercise of the various means of suggestion.

The best physicians utilize this fact in their practice. It is a common experience for a patient to feel ill and depressed when the doctor comes and after a brief talk in which the physician has appealed to the patient's sense of humor, has spoken with confident optimism of recovery, and otherwise sowed positive seeds of hope, the patient has found himself feeling much better and substantial progress has been made toward actual recovery. Such is the power of one mind over another mind as well as directly over the body.

If we would contribute to the well being of those with whom we associate, we should always cultivate the habit of cheerfulness, the habit of laughter, the habit of positive optimistic thinking, which excludes doubts and fears. The highest degree of health of body and health of mind is possible only as we make self-control an established habit of our lives. Every man is weakened physically, mentally and morally every time he yields to passion, however trying conditions may be, and we suffer ourselves to yield an advantage by giving way to anger. Complete health is comprehensive of all that pertains to the life of man.

## Other Cures Without Drugs

Under this subject might properly be considered many simple home remedies that are used successfully in the treatment of diseases. These, however, are treated in another chapter under the title, Simple Home Remedies. We might also discuss nursing, for cures are accomplished more through good nursing than through the use of drugs. Indeed, nursing is almost always the principal thing. This will be considered in the chapter on Nursing. Still another very important matter remains to be taken up in this chapter. It is the use of water.

———

The only way for a rich man to be healthy is by exercise and abstinence; to live as if he were poor.
—[Temple.

The surest road to health, say what they will,
Is never to suppose we shall be ill.
—[Churchill.

For 'tis the mind that makes the body rich.
—[Shakespeare.

# WATER TREATMENT

BATHING and the use of water in other ways to promote health is so beneficial that the subject deserves special attention. Water has four qualities that need to be considered: moisture, temperature, impact and as a solvent. The moisture relaxes and absorbs, according to the temperature and the degree and time of its confinement upon a surface. Its evaporation cools or chills. It loosens to the extent of its absorption by any tissue. Cold applications, by the abstraction of heat from the body, drive the blood from the surface, thus constricting the blood vessels and contracting the tissues to which the applications are made. If the cold application is soon removed, the blood returns with such force as to expand the blood vessels to a greater extent than before, and increases the quantity of blood there. This increases the nutrition, and has a tonic effect. If the cold application is continued the abstraction of heat goes on and vitality is lessened.

## Degrees of Heat

If the application is tepid—from 70 to 85 degrees —it relaxes the skin and extremities of the nerves and thus becomes soothing. The application of warmth and moisture tends to loosen the fiber of the structures and causes relaxation which favors both secretion and excretion, but the quality of the secretions may be poorer than normal.

If the application is hot—from 95 degrees to 100 degrees—it stimulates, because it brings an abnormal degree of heat in contact with the surface, and contributes to the internal heat that cannot escape. In acute conditions it is often an excellent general stimulant. If the application is quickly removed, the effect is only that of a local stimulant, generally applied. If the application is continued, it causes muscular contraction. If continued over a large extent of surface, the hot application may cause faintness before the stimulation has given place to contraction, because the rush of blood to the surface partially empties the large blood vessels, including those of the brain.

If the application is warm—from 85 degrees to 95 degrees—it has, to a modified degree, the effect of a hot application. There is dilation of the blood vessels of the skin, relaxation, copious perspiration, quickened pulse and respiration, but with a slight general decrease of temperature. The warm application continued has a weakening effect. The alternation of hot and cold applications in quick succession increases circulation, warmth and vigor.

## Impact and Solvency

Impact, or water applied with force, arouses nervous action, and calls the blood to the surface. Its effect is dependent upon the degree of force; the temperature of the water and the condition of the system. Concerning the solvent properties of water, that is, the power to dissolve substances, hot water possesses them to a greater degree than cold. Pure water is more solvent than impure. The solvent power may be increased by the addition of certain other things.

## Temperament Makes a Difference

In the use of water in the treatment of disease there are special peculiarities of the person treated to be considered. In the matter of temperament, the sanguine can bear lower temperatures than others; the bilious are hard to affect, and hence need more heroic treatment. The nervous temperament requires short applications with frequent changes; the lymphatic are slow to react, and are particularly liable to be injured by the injudicious use of water. If one is not quite sure how he should be classified as to temperament, it is necessary to carefully experiment at the beginning of any water treatment. There is not only the matter of temperament to be considered, but also any special derangement that may exist in the various organs of the body, and the general condition as to vitality. In the matter of baths, time and temperature should be carefully regulated to the disease and strength of the patient.

## Effects Direct and Indirect

Every bath has an immediate and local effect, and a remote constitutional effect. The constitutional effects are indirect, working toward improved nutrition, equalized circulation, with normal temperature and properly performed functions of the various organs; also the highest possible degree of general vigor.

Always use pure, soft water when possible. The bath should be discontinued as soon as the desired effect is realized; too little effect is better than too great. In the treatment of disease through baths, repetition is important. In chronic cases, the second bath should be given before the constitutional effect is lost; in acute cases, before the local effect of the first is lost.

## Wet Packs

Wet packs are used in the treatment of some diseases, the temperature ranging from hot to cold, usually with the purpose of inducing perspiration. In whole packs, the patient is wrapped completely in a sheet or blanket wrung out of hot water, and is then rolled in woolen blankets. The cold pack is used to reduce temperature in fevers. Packs may be used to apply to a single limb, or part of the body. The spinal pack is sometimes applied to relieve lumbago, reduce fever and remove congestion. Abdominal packs are used in acute indigestion and cramps. Compresses are similar to packs, but usually consist of cloth folded to a thickness of half an inch or more wet in water and applied to the surface like a bandage.

## Compresses

Ice cold compresses blunt the sensibility of the nerve, and influence reflex nervous functions, often having a pronounced effect upon the circulation of internal organs. They relieve pain, the delirium of fevers; are useful for hemorrhage and local inflammation. Cold over the spine relieves muscular spasms, lessens muscular sensibility and secretions and raises body heat elsewhere. Some of the results are obtained by cold compresses upon the back of the neck at the base of the brain. Chest compresses are useful in bronchial and lung congestions and pleurisy.

## Vapor Baths

Water is useful in the treatment of some diseases, especially those of the respiratory organs, in the form of vapor. Vapor baths may be either clear water or medicated. They open the pores, aid in elimination and cause muscular relaxation.

## Foot and Sitz Baths

Partial baths are often beneficial, especially the foot baths and sitz baths. A cold foot bath should be quickly taken, the time being from one to three minutes. It draws the blood from the head and chest, and has a hardening effect, promoting rest and sleep. A warm foot bath, lasting from twelve to fifteen minutes, relieves congestion, correcting the circulation, and is useful for the weak, nervous or those having poor blood. A handful of salt improves it. The hot foot bath helps to break up colds, and relieves congestion. It should be taken quickly.

The sitz bath is taken by simply sitting in a small tub of water coming well up above the hips and thighs as seated. The cold sitz bath strengthens the organs of the lower part of the body, and has a general invigorating effect. The time should be from two to three minutes. The warm sitz bath should be from two to fifteen minutes, and is good for constipation, colic and the conditions requiring relaxation. The hot sitz bath may be given to relieve acute conditions of the organs of the lower part of the body, especially those due to deranged circulation of the blood. The time for this bath is about five minutes.

# NURSING

IF you ask a good doctor for his opinion of nursing, he is likely to to be frank enough to admit that nursing is usually more important than doctoring. The doctor tells the nurse what to do, but the nursing is the thing. People are always influenced more or less by their surroundings. This is especially true in sickness. The patient is more sensitive to environment than when well, and the mind naturally dwells upon the visible environment much of the time because not otherwise occupied. The sick room should be clean and so arranged as to have a neat, orderly appearance, with no superfluous furniture and hangings upon which the dust may accumulate. There should be something of the ornamental present; a few flowers, which should be removed at night, have a cheering effect.

Ventilation is very important and the patient should be provided with good air to breathe at all times. The room should not be overheated nor should it be allowed to become damp and cold to the point of discomfort. It is almost always perfectly safe to breathe cold air, but there should be sufficient covering over the body to prevent chill. On the other hand, care should be taken that no more coverings are used than are really necessary.

The weight and heat of unnecessary bed coverings have a depressing effect and lower the vitality.

Except in diseases where it is necessary to have the room darkened, sunshine should enter the sick room every day the sun shines. Care should be taken that there is no constant glare of light, especially around the sick bed. Loud or disagreeable noises within the hearing of the patient should be eliminated so far as possible. Quiet should be maintained in the room to the extent of refraining from unnecessary clatter and loud or excited talking; but, on the other hand, never whisper in a sick room; let the conversation be carried on in low, quiet tones. At the same time act and talk naturally, and dispel as far as possible any evidence of worry or anxiety. Whispering stirs the imagination and contributes to the fears of the patient.

## The Atmosphere of Good Cheer

Every effort should be made to appear cheerful in the presence of the patient, and the humorous side of things should be presented. An occasional laugh will do the patient much good. The most important thing for a sick room is that mysterious, yet positively pervading condition we call atmosphere. The rooms should have an atmosphere of good cheer. The nurse should appear neatly but simply dressed, and should always give special attention to personal cleanliness. She should not fuss with the patient nor do any unnecessary tending which might cause nervousness in the patient.

While it is wise to consult the patient's wishes in matters in which it is safe to follow his wishes, in general, a nurse should do her work in a positive but gentle way, without hesitation or questioning.

Great care should be taken to avoid any disagreement with the patient.

## Bathing

It is an almost invariable rule that a patient should be bathed daily. A cleansing bath in the morning, with an alcohol rub at night, should be given, devoting especial attention to the back, dusting it after the rub with talcum powder and keeping bed linen clean and smooth lest the skin becomes irritated and bed sores result. The patient's mouth should be kept clean, using some good antiseptic solution.

In special details of nursing the directions of a physician should be sought and carefully followed.

## SURGERY

Modern surgery has accomplished many wonderful things. Many diseases and conditions due to disease or accident that were formerly regarded as incurable have been cured through the methods devised in connection with modern surgery. One of the chief reasons for this success is that an attempt is made to secure absolute cleanliness in connection with all surgical operations. It is the purpose of the modern surgeon to have not only the part of the body operated upon, but the instruments and everything near the patient, clean; not only in the sense that we usually understand that word, but sterile—free from living germs of any kind.

This is an important thing to remember in the treatment of all injuries and sores. Absolute cleanliness and freedom from germs make it much easier and quicker for nature to perform its functions of healing. It is not the medicine used that heals, but nature itself.

## How to Dress a Wound

If a wound has been received, the skin about it should be thoroughly scrubbed with soap and water and the wound itself cleansed with a solution of boracic acid as strong as can be made, or with creolin, a teaspoonful to a pint of boiled water. Then the edges of the wound should be brought together, using a strip of zinc oxide plaster, if necessary, and some sterilized bandages. This dressing should not be disturbed for several days, unless heat, pain and swelling are present.

## To Stop Bleeding

In case of bleeding from an artery, which will be recognized by a spurting from the blood vessel with each impulse of the heart, compression of the limb should be made above the wound—that is, nearer the heart. In case of a large artery, a handkerchief can be loosely tied about the limb and a stick inserted and twisted until the bleeding stops. In case of bleeding from the veins, the blood flows steadily without any intermission or spurting. Here cording of the limbs is unnecessary.

After cleaning the wound apply a dressing of gauze, a folded napkin, or any clean piece of cloth, and cover with a tight bandage.

If the bleeding comes from a part of the body where no bandage can be applied, pressure of the blood vessel against a neighboring bone may stop the bleeding.

When bleeding is stopped by pressure, clots of blood form very rapidly and block up the injured blood vessels in ordinary cases. There are several substances which, applied to a wound, help to thicken the blood and check the flow. Among them are tannic acid and alum. Table salt is also effective. Blood vessels are contracted by cold, and cold water will sometimes stop bleeding. It is always best to avoid the use of drugs for such cases if relief can be obtained by bandaging or other pressure.

## Nose Bleed

Bleeding from the nose can usually be stopped by cold applications and firm pressure with the fingers upon the sides of the nose. A pad beneath the upper lip with pressure from without may also help to shut off the blood supply. For hemorrhage of the stomach absolute quiet should be maintained and pieces of ice may be swallowed.

In all serious cases of bleeding, from whatever cause, a doctor should be called as soon as possible. and it is only pending his arrival that every possible means is taken to check the flow of blood.

## Fractures

No attempt should be made in most cases to set a broken bone by anyone who does not know how. If the bones broken are badly out of place, it is sometimes best to bring the ends of the bones as near together as possible by carefully pulling a broken leg or arm. Ordinarily, a bone may be set several days after it is broken, with satisfactory results. The most serious complications attending fractures are those resulting from the laceration of the flesh. In these so-called compound fractures, the broken bone may be forced through the flesh and brought through the skin. In case of such wounds, they should be thoroughly disinfected with antiseptics; otherwise, let alone, as there is great danger of infection.

Inasmuch as swelling rapidly follows a fracture and makes the setting of the bone difficult, it is important that a surgeon should be called at once. This is especially urgent in the case of compound fractures. While awaiting the surgeon, the patient should be placed in as comfortable a position as possible and kept quiet. If it is necessary to move him, improvised splints, which may be any smooth sticks or small pieces of board, may be applied to steady the limb, so that the injured part may not suffer unnecessarily from moving. The splints should be padded in some way, if possible, and should be bound firmly to the limb. Care should be taken not to have pressure at the point of fracture.

In setting a broken bone it is necessary that the ends be brought together properly; otherwise, they grow together crooked or short. The bones of the leg unite in from six to eight weeks. Those of the forearm in from four to five weeks, collar bone in about four weeks, ribs in about three weeks, the small bones of the hands in from two to three weeks. This is in the case of the average adult. The bones of the aged are slower in uniting or may not unite solidly at all. The bones of children unite more quickly than those of adults.

## MEDICAL AND SURGICAL AIDS

There should be a well-stocked home medicine chest or a cupboard set apart where can be quickly found medical and surgical aids for use in emergencies. This is needed in every home, but it is especially important for persons living on farms or ranches where it is difficult to get a doctor quickly. The bottles and packages should be plainly labeled. Some of the things that it is desirable to have are the following:

Graduated medicine glass, medicine dropper, hot water bag, fountain syringe, fever thermometer, absorbent cotton, gauze bandages or thoroughly sterilized long strips of white cotton cloth, surgeons' plaster, caustic pencil, spirits of ammonia, chloride of lime, sulphur, turpentine, tincture of iodine, crystals of permanganate of potash, boracic acid, dioxygen, creolin, calendula, arnica, spirits of camphor, vaseline, bicarbonate of soda, limewater, sweet spirits of niter, quinine pills, epsom salts, olive oil, castor oil, alcohol, French brandy, pure whisky.

---

O woman! In our hours of ease
Uncertain, coy and hard to please,
And variable as the shade
By the light quivering aspen made;
When pain and anguish wring the brow,
A ministering angel thou!

—[Scott.

# OBSTETRICAL NURSING

A PHYSICIAN should be consulted in the early stages of pregnancy, and should direct the care and habits during this period. Arrangements to secure a nurse thoroughly trained in maternity cases should be made early, several months in advance. The nurse will be able to give information about the articles required and arrangements to be made for the confinement.

## Rules for Prospective Mother

Attention should be given to the following points: Daily exercise for an hour or two in the open air, good hygienic surroundings, and at least eight hours' sleep during the twenty-four are essential; clothing loose enough to allow of free circulation of the blood; frequent bathing, a tepid sitz bath' being employed when the full bath proves too exhausting; a generous but not too stimulating diet, and rigid regularity in eating should be adhered to. The bowels, if not properly regulated by food and exercise, should be moved daily either by enema or simple laxative.

The urine should, if possible, be examined at frequent intervals during pregnancy, and at least four times during the last two months; this is of great importance to the patient and must not be neglected. The purpose is to find out if there are indications of kidney disease, which may develop during this period. The nipples require preparation or toughening. A daily application of a solution of borax—

a tablespoonful to one pint of water—can be used, and cacao butter used for lubrication.

## Fixing the Date

The date at which the birth is likely to occur can be calculated in a variety of ways, one of the simplest being to add seven days to the date of beginning of the last menstrual period and count forward nine months. This is usually within a few days of the correct time, although an occasional mistake occurs.

## The Room

A large, well-ventilated room, free from sewer connections, having, if possible, a southern exposure, should be chosen. This room and its contents should be thoroughly cleansed from dust and other impurities, and if obliged to retain old upholstered furniture and draperies, cover them, if possible, with clean sheets. Be sure that no contagious disease germs are present.

## Things Needed

Prepare a sanitary pad about three feet square. In making it, take a piece of oiled paper of this size and cover with a thick layer of cotton waste; place it between cheesecloth and tack the whole loosely about the edges with long stitches. The sanitary napkins are similarly made, except the paper. They should be of two sizes, those to be used immediately after delivery being much wider and longer than those used subsequently. The cheesecloth can be cut about twenty-five inches square and filled one-third its width and a little less than its length with cotton waste. The gauze is then folded over and stitched down the center and across the ends.

The smaller napkin is made in the same way, except that it should be much narrower and the cotton waste should extend only about ten inches of its length, thus leaving the ends free and firm for pinning. Both the pads and napkins can be sterilized by placing them in a covered dish or between two pans in an oven and subjecting them to a slow heat for about four or five hours. Avoid exposing them to the air till ready for use.

### Preparing the Bed

The bed should be made by covering the mattress first with a clean sheet and then with a rubber sheet or tar paper. The latter is inexpensive and should be burned after use. Over this spread a second sheet, and then another rubber sheet, about a yard wide, covering the middle of the bed and tucked firmly in at the sides. Then put in place the " sanitary pad," or, in the absence of this, sheets folded in four or more thicknesses to absorb the discharge.

### The Beginning of Labor

The beginning of labor is indicated by pains in the lower part of the abdomen and back, occurring at regular intervals about once every half hour, and a discharge of mucus, tinged with blood from the vagina. True pains can be distinguished from those that are false by placing the hand over the lower part of the abdomen; in true pains the contractions of the uterus are to be readily felt through the abdominal wall. As labor advances the pains grow more severe and the intervals shorter. The first stage of labor consists in the dilation of the uterus and ends when the uterus is completely dilated. The second stage, or stage of expulsion, ends when the child is born. The third stage ends when the placenta is discharged and the uterus well contracted.

## Cleanliness of Nurse

The nurse should have an entire change of her personal clothing, and should always wear, while on duty, washable dresses and aprons, keeping herself scrupulously clean. During the child-bearing stage a woman is particularly susceptible to infection, and it is almost criminal to undertake the care of a woman about to be confined after being in contact with any disease, either contagious or septic, that is communicable.

## First Stage of Labor

In the first stage of labor the patient should be allowed to walk about, or sleep if inclined to do so. The large intestine is made perfectly free of any accumulation of fecal matter by an enema. This makes the labor easier and sometimes shortens its duration. Simple fluids should be given, avoiding alcoholic or other stimulants. The patient must be instructed not to bear down during the pains of this stage, and to sit if walking about when a pain occurs. There is danger of too early rupture of the membranes and protracted and painful labor in consequence.

## Ready for the Doctor

Have ready for the examination by the doctor hot water, soap, two clean nail brushes and two bowls, one containing a disinfectant solution. Before preparing the patient for the examination the hands and forearms of the attendant should be scrubbed for three minutes in hot soap suds with a stiff nail brush and washed again in a disinfectant solution. The nails should be kept short and care taken not to roughen them. Use for cleaning a bone or a wood cleaner, and prevent the roughening of the skin of the hands by the use of glycerin and by wiping them perfectly dry.

The patient should be dressed in a loose wrapper and placed on the back at the right side of the bed, with the clothes drawn out of the way and two sheets adjusted, one over each leg, to protect the body during examination. After scrubbing the hands, clean carefully the external genitals and surrounding parts of the patient with soap and water and afterward with sterilized water or disinfectant solution, and remember that the hands should always be held in a disinfectant each time before touching the genitals if they have handled other articles not sterilized.

## The Second Stage

During the second stage the patient must be put to bed and not allowed to leave it for any purpose. She should be covered by a sheet folded and tied loosely about the waist by a tape passed through the middle and fastened securely to the nightgown, which can be gathered in soft folds well under the arm. Strong safety pins should be used to pin the sheet, which is lapped over the right side so as to cover both legs; the feet should be enveloped in a pair of white cotton stockings.

## Assistance at Delivery

Delivery is usually made with the patient lying upon the left side, but some practitioners prefer the patient placed upon the back. Firm pressure made upon the lower part of the back during the pains gives relief (in doing this the hand of the attendant should be kept clean by using a disinfected towel), and the patient may be allowed to pull on a sheet firmly secured to the foot of the bed. This greatly increases the expulsive power of the uterus, and must be avoided in rapid delivery; otherwise, the parts may be ruptured.

In the third stage the person assisting may be called upon to hold the uterus by placing the hand upon the abdominal wall and watching to see that it remains properly contracted. Sometimes it becomes necessary to make circular movements over the uterus or to grasp it, and pushing firmly downward promote contractions till the placenta, which should always be kept for the doctor's inspection, is delivered.

## If the Doctor Is Not Present

In emergency, when no doctor is present, the patient should be placed on the left side with the knees flexed. All antiseptic precautions being taken, the vaginal outlet should be carefully watched.

When the head is to be seen, place the fingers against it and hold it back during the pains, to prevent too rapid expulsion and to allow the gradual stretching of the vaginal floor. If this plan be faithfully carried out, there is little danger of laceration. With the first child the labor is often slow, two hours or more being required for the passage of the head. In subsequent labor the time is usually about an hour. If the head is coming too rapidly, tell the patient to open her mouth and avoid bearing down.

When the head is delivered, insert the finger into the passage to see if the cord be about the neck, and if so pull it carefully over the head and wipe the eyes and mouth free from secretion. The hand should then be placed on the abdomen over the uterus, moved downward until the child is expelled, and still held firmly till the placenta is expressed and the uterus contracted. The placenta should be twisted as it is expelled till all the membranes come away.

## Aid to Contraction

The uterus should be held until contraction is firm. The pulse should be taken frequently, and, if it becomes very rapid, the physician should be called at once, as this probably indicates approaching hemorrhage.

As soon as the child is delivered the patient can be turned on the back and an assistant told how to watch and hold the uterus, so that attention may be given the child.

## What to Do for the Child

The child should first be made to cry out by slapping the back with the hand or a wet towel, dashing a little cold water in the face if necessary. If it fails to respond to this treatment, and is not breathing, the cord should be cut at once (it is usual to wait till pulsation has ceased). This is done by tying it with any clean, strong string about one inch from the body, and again two inches from that, and cutting between. Frequent subsequent examination of the cord is necessary to be sure no hemorrhage is taking place. The child's body should then be immersed in a hot bath at a temperature of 100° to 105° Fahr. The head should be bent backward, and a piece of gauze or a handkerchief placed over its mouth, so that air can be blown into the lungs by breathing through the covering. This should be done at least twelve or fifteen times, or till the child takes a long breath.

## Sanitary Attentions

When the child is successfully delivered, as described, the patient should be cleansed of discharges by bathing all parts either with warm water that has been boiled or with disinfectant solution, sterilized gauze or muslin that has been disinfected being used. Be very careful to resterilize the hands before touching the genitals.

When all impurities are removed, one of the sanitary napkins should be used. If not sterilized, a few layers of gauze saturated in disinfectant solution may be placed under it. The soiled pad and bedding should be removed and replaced by clean.

## The Abdominal Binder

An abdominal binder is then usually applied. This binder should be made of unbleached muslin or bleached twill. It is three feet six inches in length, and fourteen inches in width, and should, when pinned in place, extend from the border of the ribs in front to below the prominence of the hips. It should be made to fit perfectly the contour of the body by taking in darts above and below. To this is fastened the sanitary napkin held in place by four large safety pins.

The abdominal binder should be changed as often as soiled. It is usually worn about seven days, although its use may be continued longer if comfort is derived from it.

## Rest and Recuperation

The general rules for the care of medical cases apply to obstetrical nursing as well. During the first week or more, visitors should be excluded, as rest and quiet are of much importance. The patient should be kept on her back for the first six or seven hours, after which she should be raised into a sitting position to empty the bladder. If unable to urinate, a catheter should be used. Afterward, the position should be frequently changed. In some cases, the freedom of the room is allowed within ten days, and many women who are strong resume their usual routine of life at the end of three weeks. Too great haste in this matter is often regretted afterward when some uterine difficulty traceable to carelessness at this time appears.

## Cleanliness

The bed, the patient and the room must be kept perfectly clean. Some doctors allow a bath every second day. The greatest possible care should be used in giving it that the patient may not be chilled. The napkin will have to be changed at first every hour, and later every three to five hours, the parts being thoroughly cleansed and kept free from odor.

All soiled clothes must be removed at once; the napkin can be wrapped in paper and burned immediately.

## Diet and the Bowels

The diet is usually liquid for the first twenty-four hours, and if all symptoms are normal after that a full meat diet is often allowed.

The bowels are usually moved on the third day by an enema or glycerin suppository, or other medication by mouth. Medicine or vaginal douches should be given only when ordered by the physician.

## Care of Breasts

The breasts also require careful management. The nipples should be cleansed after every nursing with some weak boracic acid solution, to prevent cracking and infection. If the breasts become too full give fluid sparingly, and apply a bandage for compression, or rub very carefully with the hands from the base toward the nipple, the motion being circular. Rubbing is not advised where inflammation is present.

---

Nothing begins, and nothing ends,
   That is not paid with moan;
For we are born in other's pain,
   And perish in our own.

—[Thomson.

# The  Baby

ETTING ready for the first baby is a task involving so much work and so many things, according to modern ideas, that it takes a whole book to tell all about it. Some of the most important things needed at the time of the birth **are** usually brought by the physician. It is a good plan, however, to have on hand and ready for use most of the things that are sure to be needed. Great care should be taken to have everything perfectly clean. Among the articles desirable are the following: Several hand towels, braided silk or a skein of bobbin for tying the cord, a fountain syringe, two china or porcelain basins, a bed pan, a small package of absorbent cotton, a can of sterile gauze, bichloride tablets, powdered boracic acid, olive oil, a large oilcloth, eight yards of nursery cloth for pads, unbleached muslin for binders, two yards long and 18 inches wide, and large safety pins. Have plenty of hot water at the time of confinement.

Now for the baby's equipment. It is hardly necessary to enumerate the articles of clothing needed. For the care of the baby a basket should be prepared and equipped with the following articles: A complete set of clothes, a woolen shawl or shoulder blanket, two soft towels, an old **soft** blanket in which to receive the child after birth, a fine soft sponge and a soft washcloth, white castile soap, a box of talcum powder, vaseline, boracic acid, a baby's soft hair brush, blunt-pointed scissors, safety pins of assorted sizes, and absorbent cotton.

## The Bath

The health of the baby depends in a large degree upon its bath. Soon after the baby is born it should be given its first bath. It should be with warm olive oil applied with a large wad of cotton. This serves the purpose of not only cleansing the skin, but leaves just enough oil so that chilling of the body is prevented. A sponge bath should be given daily until the navel cord has dried and fallen off, which usually occurs between the fourth and eighth days. Then tub baths should be given.

The baby's bath should always be given in a warm room, the temperature being 75 and 80 degrees above zero. A bath thermometer should be used to make sure of the water temperature, which should be between 98 and 100 degrees, and the bathtub should be so placed as to avoid drafts of air. In preparation for the bath the baby should be undressed, and, resting in the lap of the nurse, should be carefully washed with fresh water, using the bath cloth. Before bathing the body, the face and head should be thoroughly dried. Then the entire body may be carefully bathed with castile soap and water, keeping the baby wrapped in the flannel blanket as much as possible while this is being done.

Then place him gently in a bath tub and thoroughly wrinse off all soap. He should then be placed on warm towels and these should be wrapped around him and gently manipulated until he is dry. Another towel should be used, to be sure of drying all the little folds of flesh under the arms, at the neck and between the thighs. A little alcohol rub may then be given, and talcum powder should be dusted on the neck, behind the ears, under the arms and knees and around the upper parts of the legs. Wipe away the superfluous powder, that it may not irritate the skin.

As the baby grows older the temperature of the bath should be lowered, and at a year old 85 to 90 degrees is warm enough. As he grows older he may remain in the water longer, and, after the morning bath, may receive a dash of cold water over his spine. This may be given with a sponge while sitting or standing in the bath water. This helps to harden the baby and prevents taking cold easily.

## Matters for Special Care

The eyes should be kept carefully cleaned by the use of a mild solution of boracic acid on absorbent cotton. The mouth also should be cleansed carefully and a little absorbent cotton wrapped around the finger may be used for this purpose.

Sometimes it is necessary to wash the mouth immediately after birth to remove mucus or other material that may be there. The scalp may need special attention if scales appear upon it. These may be removed by using a little melted cacao butter. Great care should be used in washing the scalp because of the soft spot on the top of the head. The nostrils and ears should be cleaned with a wooden toothpick over which a little absorbent cotton is twisted, care being taken that the end is completely covered with the cotton. It should be dipped in a solution of boracic acid before being used.

A safe solution of boracic acid for washing the baby's mouth may be made by dissolving a teaspoonful of the powder in a pint of boiling water, or a druggist will furnish a 2 per cent solution, which should be the strength called for for this purpose.

As a rule, the regular bath is not given in the evening, but a general alcohol rub is beneficial just before putting the baby to bed. If baby's skin shows a tendency to become red and chafed it may be best to use no soap with the bath, and bathing thoroughly may be omitted for a few days if any eruption appears upon the skin.

Absolute cleanliness is of great importance with reference to not only the baby's body but everything that comes in contact with its body. It should not only be kept clean, but dry.

## Feeding

The matter of feeding is, perhaps, the most serious problem during the first year of a child's life. It is always best for the mother and best for the baby that the child should be breast fed if conditions are normal. Conditions are such in many cases that the baby has to be fed from a bottle, and great care has to be exercised to prepare a fluid that as nearly as possible contains the same elements, in the same proportions, as does the mother's milk.

A good physician is able to prescribe a formula for the preparation of baby's food at different ages, but there is no sure rule of success in this matter, and if the food does not agree with the baby it is necessary to experiment until a preparation has been secured that is satisfactory. One of the best milk mixtures for a baby contains cow's milk, cream, limewater, sugar of milk and pure water. The formula should be obtained from a physician. The time of feeding is important. During the first four weeks feeding should be at intervals of two hours; from four weeks to three months, at intervals of two and one-half hours; from three months to one year, three hours, except at night.

After the first three months the last feeding at night should be about ten o'clock, and, if sleeping, the baby should not be disturbed to feed again until about four o'clock or even later in the morning. Many make the mistake of not giving babies enough water. They are frequently thirsty, and lukewarm water should be given them several times a day from the first. It may be given with a spoon or a nursing bottle. They may quite early be taught to drink from a cup.

### Air and Sunshine

The health of the baby depends much on sunshine and fresh air. One should not be afraid of open windows in the room where the baby sleeps either day or night. But great care should be taken to avoid a direct draft upon the child. The baby should sleep in a separate bed. He should take one or more naps each day out of doors. This is usually best arranged with his carriage upon a well-shaded piazza. The child should be sufficiently covered to be perfectly warm, with the covering so arranged that there is no obstruction to his breathing the fresh air. The carriage top should be adjusted well down to protect from the wind.

The air that the baby breathes should be purified and vitalized by sunshine, but care should be taken that the eyes are not subjected to bright light, especially during the first few weeks, and the direct rays of the sun should not strike upon the face or head. Convulsions and death sometimes result from leaving the baby where the hot sun shines directly upon it.

## The Bowels

One of the special things to watch in caring for a baby is the condition of the bowels. They are rarely perfectly regular, but the appearance of curds and highly colored matter is always a warning of digestive derangement, and suggests that care should be taken to correct the difficulty, through the diet, if possible. Any serious derangement should be reported to the family physician, and care should always be taken to avoid overfeeding.

Babies are sometimes underfed, and there is always a possibility that the mother's milk may not be sufficiently nourishing, or sufficient in quantity, or that it may lack some needed food element.

## Don't Drug Babies

Babies ought not to be drugged. Never give medicine to a nursing baby unless directed to do so by a good physician. Never administer paregoric or soothing syrup. Such preparations contain opium, and they are exceedingly dangerous. They are effective to stop crying and make the baby sleep, but often babies so dosed never awaken. One of the worst crimes against babies and a not infrequent one is the habitual use of soothing syrups and paregoric.

# MEDICINES

OUT of the hundreds of drugs and preparations of various kinds known to medical science, we have selected some of the most common. We certainly do not recommend the household use of all these things, but it is worth while to know something about them. It gives a little insight into the practice of medicine, and over the more dangerous drugs raises a warning signal. It is quite as important to know what is dangerous as what is safe. A more general knowledge of the character of drugs might save many fatalities that result from taking the wrong thing. As an example we call special attention to the following:

## HEADACHE REMEDIES

In the most dangerous class of remedies that are now used are the headache powders and tablets. Three powerful drugs are commonly used in the preparation of mixtures intended for the relief of headache and other minor aches and pains. They are acetanilid, antipyrin and phenacetin. They are coal tar products, and possess similar characteristics. These drugs were first used chiefly for the reduction of fever, but doctors came to employ them less and less for this purpose, as they learned from experience of their bad effects. They gradually came to be prescribed more and more for the relief of pain, and today they are chiefly used for this purpose. They are extensively advertised and sold for the relief of headache and other pains, largely in the form of so-called patent medicines.

The unfavorable symptoms produced by these drugs affect principally the heart and circulation, and through them other parts of the body, and are generally observed as the result of their ill-advised use in the form of medicines for the relief of headache and other forms of pain.

## The Poisoning

The symptom which occurs most frequently in poisoning by these drugs is blueness of the skin. If the dose taken has not been large, the discoloration may be very slight, and may affect only a small portion of the body; thus, in some persons who habitually use headache powders containing these drugs, all that may be noticed is an occasional blueness of the lips and mouth, and possibly of the nails and finger tips. If, however, the doses are larger, or are taken more frequently, the blueness may affect the skin of the whole body.

This is due to destructive changes in the blood, which are the direct result of the use of the drug, and are accompanied by impoverishment of the blood; hence, those who take these remedies habitually, often suffer from anæmia and the symptoms accompanying this condition—pallor, shortness of breath, palpitation of the heart, muscular weakness and disinclination to make any exertion. The injudicious use of these remedies also has a harmful effect upon the heart, thus making more pronounced the symptoms already mentioned.

## Government Sounds Warning

So many cases of poisoning, due either to overdoses or the habitual use of these drugs, and so many deaths have resulted, that the national government and many of the states have investigated this matter of headache remedies. The result of the investigation has led to the issue of special bulletins, in which the public are warned against the use of acetanilid, phenacetin and antipyrin, except as prescribed by a physician.

Attention is called to the fact that manufacturers often misrepresent the contents of headache remedies by stating upon the package that the remedy is harmless and contains no poisonous or harmful ingredients. The majority of the manufacturers comply with the law by naming upon the label the drugs used in the preparation. The claims of manufacturers of acetanilid preparations that they add nourishment for some part of the body—that is, as nerve food or brain food—are false.

## Let Them Alone

The only safe rule to follow is never to use the drugs referred to unless prescribed in a particular instance by a reliable physician. There is danger of poisoning from an overdose, and the habitual use of headache powders is practically certain to result in constitutional poisoning that will result seriously if not fatally. Acetanilid and antipyrin are more dangerous than phenacetin, but the latter possesses many of the harmful characteristics of the others, and is almost as dangerous.

## THE MEDICINE LIST

In the list of medicines that follows we have aimed simply to state the character of each, the effect upon the body and the purposes for which it is used with best results.

### ACETANILID

A coal tar preparation similar to phenacetin and antipyrin. It is given to lower temperature and relieve pain. It is a heart depressant, and its use should be only under the direction of a physician.

### ACONITE

A poisonous plant whose action is due to an alkaloid called aconitine. It lessens pain by decreasing the sensibility of the nerves. It dilates the blood vessels and causes perspiration. It may be used in drop doses of the tincture in the early stages of cold. When the skin is hot and dry and the patient is feverish and restless, it quiets the nerves, moistens the skin and reduces the fever.

### ALCOHOL

A fluid resulting from the fermentation of starch or sugar. It is the most active ingredient of intoxicating liquors. Alcohol is not a stimulant in a true sense, but a depressant. It is a good antiseptic and is valuable for bathing when applied with rubbing and massaging in cases of weakness and disease.

## ALOES

A plant of the lily family, the dried juice of the leaves being used for chronic constipation. It is very bitter and stimulates the flow of bile and other movements of the digestive tract. It is given in combination with aromatic substances. Alone it causes pain.

## ALUM

A mineral substance usually formed in the manufacture of coal gas. Applied to the mucous membrane, it causes puckering and thickening, and diminishes secretion. It checks bleeding. Solutions of alum are used for mouth washes, and dried alum applied to canker sores destroys the germs and helps in healing. In large doses it is poisonous

## AMMONIA

A volatile gas with an extremely irritating odor, which, in solution, is an alkaloid caustic that will burn the mucous membrane. Diluted, the solution is used as smelling salts, which stimulates the mucous membrane of the nose and helps, indirectly, to stimulate the heart action in cases of fainting or poisoning. It is applied to insect bites to relieve the irritation. Aromatic spirits of ammonia are used as a heart stimulant. It must be well diluted to prevent poisoning.

## AMYL NITRITE

A volatile oily liquid prepared from alcohol which, in the form of vapor, greatly stimulates heart action by causing dilation of the blood vessels. It is usually used for inhalation in attacks of angina pectoris and epileptic attacks and other diseases which cause acute contraction of the blood vessels. Its action is very quick and soon passes away.

## ANISE

The fruit of a plant containing volatile oil, used to relieve colic by its effect of causing contraction and the expulsion of acids.

## ANTIPYRIN

A compound of certain coal tar products relating to the alkaloids which have the effect of relieving neuralgia, pains and spasmodic conditions of the muscles. It also reduces the temperature because of its drying effect on the mucous membrane. It is used frequently for colds in the head and chronic catarrh. It is used in headache remedies, and for many purposes in which the relief of pain is sought; also to produce sleep. It is very dangerous for persons with weak hearts, because of its distressing effect on the heart action, and it should never be taken except in serious conditions when prescribed by a physician.

## ARNICA

A plant, the tincture of which is used as a local and internal remedy in sprains and bruises, and is valuable as an internal treatment of nose bleed and other veinous hemorrhages.

## ARSENIC

A mineral poison. It is used internally in the treatment of various skin diseases, including

eczema; also for certain forms of facial neuralgia.
It is given for St. Vitus dance, anæmia, malaria
and as a tonic. For the latter purpose it is usually
combined with iron. It should never be used except as prescribed by a physician, because of its
very poisonous nature.

## ASAFETIDA

A gum obtained from a plant having the property
of stimulating the intestines and relieving colic
caused by intestinal gases. It is sometimes used
as an enema for this purpose. It stimulates the
nervous system, and it is sometimes used for
hysteria.

## BALSAM OF PERU

The balsam from a Peruvian tree used in the
treatment of wounds and ulcers and other sores. It
relieves inflammation and thus stimulates the healing processes.

## BALSAM OF TOLU

Similar to balsam of Peru, but milder and less
irritating. It is used internally for chronic inflammation of the mucous membrane.

## BEARBERRY

Uva ursi, or bearberry leaves, are used as an
astringent and a stimulant in the treatment of diseases of the kidneys and bladder; sometimes for
diarrhea, internal hemorrhage and chronic bronchitis.

## BELLADONNA

A preparation made from the deadly nightshade. It contains atropin, a poisonous alkaloid, which is used to relieve neuralgia, to dilate the pupil of the eye, and as an antidote for opium poisoning. Belladonna is prescribed for headaches, sore throats, whooping cough and to check secretions.

## BENZOIN

A balsam which stimulates the mucous membranes and used in the early stages of colds and mild bronchitis. Diluted in preparations of one to one hundred in water or salve, it is used for cracks in the skin.

## BISMUTH

A metallic substance, the insoluble salts of which exercise a mild astringent and protective influence upon the mucous membranes and inflamed surfaces. It is used internally for vomiting and diarrhea, and externally for eczema and other skin affections.

## BRANDY

A distilled alcoholic liquor made from grapes. It is used medicinally to revive one from fainting, drowning, exposure or exhaustion where the pulse is rapid and weak. It is more cordial to the stomach and causes more agreeable exhilaration than whisky, which is used for similar purposes.

## BROMIDE OF POTASSIUM

A compound of bromine and potash. It has a quieting effect upon the nervous system, and is given for epilepsy, delirium tremens, and various forms of insanity and neuralgia.

## BROMIDE OF SODIUM

A compound of bromine, carbonate of soda and iron; it has a quieting effect upon the nervous system, and tends to induce sleep. It is an astringent and a mild antiseptic.

## BROMINE

A liquid non-metallic element obtained from sea water and from some salt springs. It is a violent irritant, and was formerly used for the purposes for which iodine is used. It is a powerful disinfectant, but its odor is so pungent and disagreeable that it is now seldom employed.

## BROOM

Irish broom, or scoparius, is a shrub. It is beneficial in the treatment of dropsy. It increases the secretion of urine, stimulates the circulation of the blood, and depresses the nervous system. It will sometimes cure severe attacks of hiccough.

## BUCHU

Leaves of a plant used to stimulate the mucous membrane of the genito-urinary tract.

## CACAO BUTTER

The oil from the seed of cacao removed in the manufacture of chocolate. It is a mild lubricant for the skin and of nutritive value when thus applied. It is excellent as a base for suppositories.

## CAFFEIN

An alkaloid found in coffee, which stimulates the brain, causing wakefulness, and stimulates the heart and blood vessels. It causes an increase in the flow of urine. It is used in the treatment of various diseases when these results are desired. Strong coffee is an antidote for opium poisoning and is used as an antiseptic and deodorant.

## CALABAR BEAN

It is a seed of the African plant sometimes known as physostigma. It is poisonous. Calabar is used in certain disorders of the eye to contract the pupil, and is used to stimulate the action of the digestive organs for certain lung diseases, and sometimes for cholera. It is administered in powder form or tincture or extract.

## CALENDULA

The tincture is made from the fresh flowers of the marigold plant. It is used in the treatment of wounds, burns and ulcerated conditions of the skin and mucous membranes.

## CALOMEL

A mercury compound used as a cathartic. It is irritating and stimulates the muscular action of the digestive organs; causes an increase in the flow of bile, and at the same time clears out the intestines. As a powder, it is used for external treatment of various skin diseases.

## CALUMBA

The root of a tropical vine, used as a bitter cathartic. It is frequently used in combination with iron in the treatment of anæmia.

## CAMPHOR

A gum from an oriental tree. It is an irritant, and stimulates the nervous system, the action of the heart and the lungs. It is used in a solution with alcohol as a liniment for sprains and bruises and for rheumatism. It is given internally for nervous conditions, headache and to cure hiccough; also for cold in the head and diarrhea. It is usually employed in the form of spirits.

## CANTHARIDES

A Spanish fly which is dried in powder form. It is a powerful irritant. It is used externally to produce blisters, and, by counter irritation of the skin, relieves various internal diseases. Internally, it is valuable in the treatment of inflammation of the kidneys and bladder.

## CARBOLIC ACID

A dangerous, irritating poison, which is used in diluted form as an antiseptic and in strong solutions for disinfecting purposes. Because of its poisonous nature, several other preparations are preferable for use as an antiseptic.

## CASCARA SAGRADA

The bark of a tree having a resin that stimulates the digestive functions. It is used as a laxative and cathartic. It is especially useful for chronic constipation.

## CASTOR OIL

An oil obtained from the seed of the castor oil plant. It contains an acid which helps to make it effective as a cathartic. It thoroughly empties the intestines and then tends to check further discharges.

## CHALK

A mineral resembling limestone, which forms an important part of the organic matter of the bones. It is used in the treatment of diarrhea. It has a slight astringent action and tends to neutralize the acid condition of the intestines. Limewater is a weak solution of calcium hydrate which has the properties of chalk, and is used to overcome acidity in the digestive organs.

## CHAULMOOGRA

The oil from the seed of the gynocardia tree. It is used in treatment of leprosy and other chronic skin diseases.

## CHLORAL

A sleep-producing drug of a volatile and soluble nature, which has the effect of depressing all the functions of the body, especially the nervous system. It is exceedingly dangerous, because of the depressing effect upon the heart and lungs. It is prescribed for convulsions; in some cases of poisoning, and lockjaw. It is never to be given to children unless prescribed by a physician.

## CHLORATE OF POTASH

A mineral drug used as a gargle and as a mouth wash for various forms of inflammation.

## CHLOROFORM

A drug derived from chlorin and alcohol which is used as an anæsthetic, the patient losing consciousness and sensibility. Its danger is that it often causes death, due to complete muscular relaxation. Internally, it is given for intestinal colic, and in liniment is applied for muscular pains.

## CITRIC ACID

An acid found most extensively in lemon juice, but in smaller quantities in such acid fluids as oranges and strawberries. The acid itself is not so desirable to use as lemon juice. It has a stimulating effect on the kidneys. It causes irritation of the bladder. It improves the quality of the blood, and is used for rheumatism and catarrhal jaundice.

## CLAY

A kind of earth used as a basis for certain pills and ointments; saturated with antiseptics, it makes a good dressing for infected wounds or ulcers.

## CLOVES

The flower bud of an oriental tree used for its stimulating and warming effect. It is prescribed for colic, to relieve coughing, and for toothache. In the latter case, the oil is applied on cotton put into the cavity of the decayed tooth.

## CODEIN

A product of opium of an alkaloid nature, used to produce sleep, and given also to stop coughing. It is sometimes prescribed for diabetes. It is less powerful than morphine, and tends to reduce somewhat the disagreeable and dangerous effects of morphine. It is less apt to cause nausea and constipation.

## COD LIVER OIL

An oil obtained from the liver of the codfish. It contains iodine and fats. It is administered as a food that is easily assimilated; often used as an aid to nutrition, especially in cases of tuberculosis, anæmia and rickets. It tends to produce nausea because of its fishy taste, especially when the digestive tract is out of order.

## COFFEE

This well-known and popular beverage excites nerve action, particularly the brain. It is often given as an antidote in cases of opium poisoning. It is useful as a stimulant in cases of extreme fatigue and debility. The alkaloid caffein, from coffee, is used as a heart and kidney stimulant.

## COLCHICUM

A European plant containing the alkaloid colchicin. It is a valuable drug in gout and rheumatism, usually given as the wine of colchicum.

## COLD CREAM

Many preparations bearing this name are used to keep the skin, especially of the hands and face, in good condition. No other preparation quite takes the place of cold cream. Harsh and sticky applications are not desirable for keeping the skin smooth and soft. The following are recipes for cold creams that may be made at home. They are much less expensive than the cold creams sold at the drug stores. Here is one: Melt and mix together one dram each of white wax and spermaceti, and while warm add two ounces each of oil of almonds and rose water and one-half ounce of orange flower water. Beat until the mixture is of a creamy consistency. Put into small jars well covered, and set away in a cold place.

Another: Melt and mix one-half ounce each of spermaceti and white wax, one ounce each of cacao butter and lanolin and two ounces of sweet almond oil. Remove from the fire and add one dram of tincture of benzoin and two ounces of rose water. Beat until cold.

Still another: Four ounces almond oil, one ounce of spermaceti and white wax and two ounces of cucumber juice. Take a ripe cucumber, chopped fine, pound to a paste and squeeze out the juice through a jelly bag. Melt the spermaceti and white wax by putting them in a porcelain dish in a saucepan of boiling water; then add the almond oil and cucumber juice. Perfume with one-half dram of violet extract. Beat until cold.

A good lip salve is made by melting together when gently heated, one-half ounce of cacao butter and one-fourth ounce of oil of almonds, to which is added six drops of essence of lemon. This should be mixed well and poured into small molds to cool.

## COLLODION

Guncotton in solution with ether and alcohol. It is used for an airtight covering of the skin by painting upon the surface. The liquid evaporates quickly, leaving a firm, thin film. Sometimes 3 per cent of castor oil and 5 per cent of Canada turpentine are added to collodion to make the film more elastic; or one part castor oil to fifteen parts collodion may be used. Collodion is applied in the treatment of insect stings, burns, ulcers, smallpox, erysipelas and various other skin diseases. It is valuable in the treatment of sores that do not heal readily. Irritants, such as cantharides, are sometimes applied with collodion. There is great danger from fire in its use, as collodion is very inflammable.

## COPPER SULPHATE

A metal preparation known as blue vitriol. It is poisonous, irritating and used chiefly as an emetic and antiseptic. Externally, it is applied as a caustic.

## CORROSIVE SUBLIMATE

Bichloride of mercury. A mineral compound used in the treatment of various skin diseases and in syphilis. It is especially valuable as a disinfectant and sterilizing solution. It is a powerful poison, and its use should be under the direction of a physician.

## COTTON ROOT BARK

The bark when fresh is used to prepare an extract that stimulates the action of the intestines and the uterus.

## CREOLIN

A poisonous coal tar product. It is a good antiseptic and deodorant.

## CREOSOTE

An oily fluid distilled from beech wood. Its action is similar to that of carbolic acid. It is used to apply on cotton for toothache. In diluted form it is given to prevent fermentation in the stomach, and is prescribed for consumption and chronic bronchitis.

## CROTON OIL

An oil obtained from a tree in India. It is a powerful irritant and one of the quickest purgatives known. One or two drops in olive oil or butter will move the bowels almost immediately. In diluted form it is used as a counter irritant for sprains and muscular rheumatism. It is dangerous except when given under the direction of a physician.

## CUBEBS

The unripe berries have an oil which is used in bronchitis and urethral inflammations.

## DAMIANA

A plant, the fluid extract of which has stimulant, tonic and laxative properties.

## DANDELION

Preparations from the root of the dandelion, used in the treatment of dyspepsia and constipation, as a mild stimulant, which acts somewhat on the stomach and bowels.

## DIGITALIS

The tincture is made from the ripe leaves of the foxglove. It stimulates the muscles of the heart and blood vessels, thus increasing and making more regular the circulation of the blood throughout the body. It is given as a heart tonic, and, combined with other remedies, for kidney diseases.

## DOVER'S POWDERS

A compound acid of ten parts each of ipecac and opium and 80 parts of sugar of milk. It relieves pain and is given principally in dysentery and diarrhea.

## EPSOM SALTS

The salts of magnesia. They are used as a cathartic; sometimes given to reduce the amount of fluid in the body in dropsy and uremia.

## ERGOT

A fungus which forms upon the grain heads of rye. It is used chiefly to stop hemorrhage of the uterus after child birth. Its effect is to cause muscular contraction. Ergot is sometimes given for goitre, to reduce the enlargement of the thyroid gland.

## ETHER

An inflammable liquid made through the action of sulphuric acid upon alcohol. Its vapor is used as an anæsthetic. It acts similar to chloroform, but is much safer.

## FLAXSEED

The crushed seeds of flax plant are used for poultices. They contain a large amount of oil and this helps to hold the heat for a long time. Such poultices are insanitary because they encourage the increase of germs. Flaxseed tea is a cooling drink for sore throat, and inflammation of the stomach, intestines and bladder.

## FORMALDEHYDE

A gas formed by a compound of carbon, hydrogen and oxygen. It is obtained by the incomplete burning of wood alcohol. Formaldehyde solutions, known as formalin, are used as antiseptics and disinfectants. All such preparations are poisonous and of a highly irritating nature. A weak solution of from one-half to one per cent formaldehyde is used as an antiseptic wash. Because of its irritating qualities, it should be used with great caution. The most popular use of formalin is as a disinfectant by the process of fumigation. The method of using it is described elsewhere in this book under Fumigation.

## GELSEMIUM

A preparation made from the fresh roots of the yellow jasmin. It causes paralysis of the muscles, especially of the extremities. It is used in nervous headaches, the grippe and painful menstruation.

## GENTIAN

The root of the yellow gentian; is prepared in medicine for regulating digestive troubles. It is bitter, having the effect of increasing the appetite. It often relieves dyspepsia and constipation.

## GERANIUM

A preparation from this herb relieves certain forms of diarrhea. It is astringent and not irritating.

## GINGER

A plant grown in tropical countries. A tincture or extract is made from the bark. It is used to relieve menstrual cramps. It is an astringent, and used also for flavoring medicines.

## GLYCERIN

A sweet liquid obtained from fat and fixed oils. It absorbs moisture very readily and thus has the effect of drawing water from the tissues of the body applied to them. It is used with castor oil as a laxative; is applied for the relief of piles; and with a solution of borax is applied to cracked lips. On account of its drying effect it is not well to use it much upon the surface, as it tends to cause chapping.

## GOLDEN SEAL

This herb, including its root, is known also as yellow root, orange root and Indian dye. The scientific name is hydrastis. In the form of a tincture, fluid extract or infusion it is used for dyspepsia, jaundice, chronic diarrhea and as a remedy for gastric catarrh, caused by alcoholism. It is also a remedy for catarrhal inflammations of all mucous membranes. It is given as a substitute for alcoholic stimulants, and is a good general tonic.

## HENBANE

Hyoscyamus. The leaves of this plant are used in the preparation of a drug that encourages sleep, quiets the nerves, relieves certain forms of asthma when given hypodermically. It sometimes gives relief in epilepsy, in cholera and in lockjaw. It is a very powerful drug and its use should always be under the direction of a physician. Its action is similar to that of belladonna.

## HOFFMANN'S ANODYNE

A preparation of ether and alcohol used to relieve pain. It is a stimulant, and is used to relieve sleeplessness and nervous conditions, especially hysteria. It is a remedy for colic.

## HOPS

Like other bitters, hops tend to invigorate digestion. They help to quiet the nerves, and thus have a mild sleep-producing effect. In certain forms of dyspepsia they are helpful. They are among the best remedies for delirium tremens, and help to relieve the inflammation caused by bladder troubles. Applied externally in the form of a poultice mixed with vinegar, alcohol or hot water they help sometimes to relieve muscular rheumatism, toothache, bruises, colics and painful abscesses.

## ICHTHYOL

A crude oil obtained from a European rock, made up largely of the fossils of fish. The oil contains sulphur, and it is used in the treatment of erysipelas and various skin diseases. It is used in inflammations of mucous membranes and joints. It is antiseptic and stimulating.

## INDIAN HEMP

The flowering tops of an oriental tree. It is used to induce sleep in cases of pain or nervous exhaustion. In eastern countries it is used as an opiate to induce sensations similar to those produced by opium.

## IODINE

A non-metallic element obtained principally from the ashes of seaweed; also found in some minerals. It is used chiefly in solution with alcohol as a counter irritant and antiseptic. Painted upon the skin, it is used for sprains, and, diluted, it is used as a wash for infected wounds and ulcers. In smallpox, it tends to prevent pitting. It checks the spread of erysipelas in mild cases. Painted upon the gum it sometimes relieves toothache.

## IODOFORM

A drug prepared from a mixture of other drugs, including iodine, potassium bicarbonate and alcohol. It is used as a dusting powder for treatment of ulcers and lupus of the skin, and for surgical and other wounds. But it is much milder and slower in its action than many antiseptics. With olive oil, it is used as an injection for tuberculous sinuses. It has the advantage of not being irritating. Many do not care to use iodoform because of its disagreeable odor.

## IPECAC

The root of a South American herb. It is a powerful irritant and emetic. It is used in the treatment of chronic diarrhea; for tropical dysentery, and with opium, in Dover's powders, to break up a cold. It is a popular emetic for young children. It is given in half-teaspoonful doses every fifteen minutes until four doses have been taken, or vomiting has been caused. Not more than four doses should be given. It is used for poisoning, spasmodic croup and to cause expulsion of mucus. Syrup of ipecac is the form in which it is given to children. For adults small doses of wine of ipecac may relieve the nausea. Ipecac is given for hemorrhage of the stomach and uterus. It causes contraction, and it is a heart depressant. It is sometimes given for bronchitis.

## IRIS

The leaves and root of the blue flag are used chiefly as a cathartic. It regulates the liver and glands of the intestines.

## IRON

The salts of iron are used extensively to improve the quality and increase the quantity of blood. It helps to increase the red cells of the blood, which are lacking in anæmia. Preparations of iron are used to stop bleeding and discharges from the mucous membranes, being astringent. Iron causes destruction of the teeth when brought in contact with them, so it should be given through a glass tube.

## JUNIPER

Juniper berries are used in preparations for digestive stimulants. Also for catarrh of the urinary passages and for dropsy. The bruised berries are sometimes applied to relieve local pain.

## KUMISS

This preparation, and kephir, are known as milk wines. They are prepared from milk by fermenting with yeast, and are prescribed for consumption, scrofula, anæmia, chronic constipation and scurvy.

## LANOLIN

The purified fat obtained from sheep's wool. It is used as a basis for salves and, although it has a soothing effect on the skin, it has no special medical value itself. It is used for ointments containing iodine, with salicylic acid, for eczema; and with corrosive sublimate or carbolic acid for various skin diseases.

## LARKSPUR

A plant containing, among other alkaloids, delphinine. The European variety known as stavesacre is used in medicine. It has been applied externally in the form of an alcohol liniment for the relief of neuralgia. Tincture of larkspur is used to kill lice in the hair.

## LIMEWATER

A solution of lime considerably diluted with water. It is used to counteract the effects of excessive acid in the stomach and intestines. It is also given to relieve nausea. It is astringent and beneficial when applied locally for various skin diseases, as eczema and ulcers.

## MAGNESIA

A metallic element, the salts of which are used as a laxative. It tends to neutralize the acid in the digestive canal, and is used in various forms for the treatment of digestive disorders. Citrate of magnesia, in which magnesia is combined with citrate acid, is an agreeable but powerful cathartic. Magnesia is extensively used in the form of sulphate of magnesium, better known as epsom salts, as a cathartic. Its action is prompt and thorough.

## MALE FERN

The dried leaves of this plant are used for a preparation that will kill tapeworm. In rare cases it causes poisoning, but not usually when given in small quantities. Its use should always be under the direction of a physician.

## MANDRAKE

An herb known also as podophyllum. It is a slow but completely effective cathartic. It stimulates the flow of bile and the action of the intestines. It is often given in pills in combination with other drugs.

## MARSHMALLOW

An herb, the root of which is used to relieve inflammation of the mucous membrane and the respiratory, digestive and urinary organs. Poultices prepared with it are used to relieve inflammations of the skin. It is prescribed for the relief of mild catarrhal conditions in the form of a decoction or syrup, the sugar and mucilage it contains having a soothing effect.

## MENTHOL

A drug obtained from oil of peppermint. It is employed locally to relieve pain, producing a partial lack of sensation. It often relieves superficial neuralgic pains; the itching and burning pain of eczema; insect bites; superficial burns and scalds; boils and carbuncles. It sometimes relieves headache. It is usually applied by a menthol pencil rubbed upon the surface. In solution it relieves congestion of the mucous membranes of the nose and throat. It is given internally for some forms of dyspepsia.

## MERCURY

A metallic drug which, in the compound known as calomel, is used as a cathartic. Mercury is the only positive remedy for syphilis, but its use is attended by great danger, and it should be used only as directed by a physician. The drug is sometimes rubbed upon the skin and thus absorbed by the system.

## MUSK

A secretion from the musk deer of Asia. It is prescribed to relieve acute nervous disorders, especially involving spasms. It is given for nervous conditions which arise in fevers and pneumonia; also cholera infantum, whooping cough, spasmodic croup, hiccough, cholera and sometimes lockjaw and hysteria. It is not only quieting, producing refreshing sleep, but is at the same time stimulating and tends to prevent collapse. The drug is very expensive.

## MYRRH

A resinous gum from an Arabian tree. It is a stimulant and tonic, and in small doses tends to improve the appetite and digestion. In some forms of anæmia it is prescribed in a mixture of iron. It is also given for chronic bronchitis.

## MORPHINE

An alkaloid obtained from opium. It is used to cause sleep and to relieve pain. It should never be given to children. It is a dangerous drug, and should be given only when prescribed by a physician. Its repeated use may lead to formation of the drug habit.

## NAPHTHALIN

This is a coal tar product, which is a powerful antiseptic. It is used to prevent putrefaction in wounds and ulcers. It does not irritate surrounding skin or exposed tissues. It is also used to prevent fermentation, and is given in some forms of diarrhea.

## NITRATE OF SILVER

Fused nitrate of silver, or lunar caustic, is a preparation of silver, nitrate acid and boric acid; is given internally to relieve various stomach disorders which occur in diarrhea and cholera. It is also prescribed for epilepsy. Externally, it is applied to cancerous and other ulcers, burns, erysipelas, and it is sometimes used in the treatment of diphtheria, croup, laryngitis. Diluted to 1 per cent, it is used to cleanse the eyes of new-born infants. It is astringent and antiseptic, and a powerful caustic. It is used as a caustic in the treatment of warts, corns and callouses. It is poison and should be used with great caution.

## NUX VOMICA

A poisonous drug containing strychnine prepared from the seeds of a tree that grows in East India. In small doses it stimulates the digestive organs. It also makes more active the circulation and respiration and renders sight and hearing more acute. It is frequently prescribed as a bitter tonic. The drug is very poisonous and dangerous except in the hands of a good physician.

## OLIVE OIL

The oil of ripe olives, also known as sweet oil. It is used as an important article of food and acts as a mild laxative for infants. It stimulates the flow of bile. It is soothing and effective as an enema. It is applied to relieve the pain of insect bites and stings, also burns.

## OX GALL

Dried bile from cattle. It is prepared in the form of a pill or enemas to relieve constipation, and the flow of bile.

## OXYGEN

The gas which forms an important part of the atmosphere, and through the processes of breathing is taken up by the blood, furnishing a necessary element of the body. Oxygen is used for medical purposes by inhalation in pneumonia and other diseases attended by difficult breathing. It is administered for poisoning from breathing illuminating gas. It is sometimes mixed with ether, chloroform and laughing gas, when these are used as anæsthetics, to lessen their ill effects. It is sometimes used in severe cases of anæmia.

## PANCREATIN

An extract prepared from the pancreas of cattle or pigs. It is used for aiding intestinal digestion.

## PAREGORIC

A tincture of opium and camphor. It is frequently used to quiet young children and many deaths are thus caused. It should never be given to children except when in acute conditions a physician prescribes it. It has the familiar properties of opium of causing sleep and relieving pain. It is sometimes given to relieve colic, but its use to check the discharges of diarrhea is a dangerous practice. It should never be used to induce sleep.

## PENNYROYAL

The leaves of this herb are used to make a hot infusion that helps to relieve congestion of the intestines caused by diarrhea. It is used to relieve inflammation of the throat, also muscular rheumatism. It is sometimes given to bring on retarded or suspended menstruation. Its use for such purposes is exceedingly dangerous, frequently causing fatal poisoning.

## PEPPER

Pepper berries dried and ground is a common product. It is a powerful stimulant and irritant.

It is used medicinally as a counter irritant and for the relief of intermittent fever. In the latter case it is combined with quinine. Pepper is sometimes used in gargles, in poultices and for the relief of muscular rheumatism, headache and colic.

## PEPPERMINT

An herb used in flavoring. Medicinally, it is used to relieve colic. The oil of peppermint is sometimes applied for the relief of neuralgia, toothache and rheumatic pains. If allowed to remain long upon the skin the oil may cause blisters. It is, therefore, best to remove it as soon as the burning sensation is pronounced, and to apply a soothing oil or vaseline.

## PEPSIN

The digestive element of the gastric juice. The medicinal preparation is obtained from the stomach of a pig, sheep or calf. It promotes the digestion of albuminous foods, including eggs and meat. It is usually prepared with hydrochloric acid, and is prescribed for digestive disorders due to a lack of pepsin in the gastric juice. In some cases it is used to start the process of digestion in foods before they are swallowed.

## PERMANGANATE OF POTASH

An alkaline antiseptic. Solutions are applied externally in fetid conditions of cancer and other abscesses, ulcers and gangrene. As a wash it is used to purify foul breath due to decayed teeth or unhealthy secretions of the throat, and for unpleasant odors from the feet or armpits. Used in strong solution it is the best local application to overcome the poisonous effects of snake bites.

## PEROXIDE OF HYDROGEN

A combination of hydrogen and oxygen which undergo a chemical change. It is a valuable agent for cleansing abscesses and ulcers, and for gargles in diphtheria and tonsilitis. It is used for bleaching the hair and removing powder stains.

## PHENACETIN

A drug resembling acetanilid obtained from coal tar. It is given to reduce fever and to relieve pain, especially in neuralgia. It is powerful and dangerous, having a depressing effect upon the heart. Its use should be avoided.

## PHOSPHORUS

A non-metallic element obtained from beans. It is a valuable drug in the treatment of rickets, nervous debility and pneumonia.

## PILOCARPIN

An alkaloid from the leaves of japorandi, a South American plant. It causes profuse perspiration and somewhat stimulates the kidneys. It is used in dropsy and other diseases to reduce the amount of fluid in the system. It greatly increases the flow of saliva and sometimes other secretions. It stimulates the circulation by diluting the blood vessels. In some eye troubles it is used to contract the pupil.

## POMEGRANATE

The bark, root and trunk of a small tree in Asia. The rind of the pomegranate fruit is used to expel tapeworms. The drug contains tannin. The rind is astringent, and is used for chronic diarrhea and ulcers of the rectum.

## PUMPKIN SEED

An extract of pumpkin seed is one of the most effective preparations used to dislodge tapeworms. About two hours after administering it a dose of castor oil is usually given.

## QUASSIA

A bitter root from the West Indies. It is prescribed as a tonic and relieves sudden attacks of indigestion. Enemas of the infusion are used for threadworms.

## QUININE

An alkaloid obtained from cinchona, a name applied to the bark of certain Peruvian trees. It is used medicinally in the form of quinine sulphate most frequently. It kills the germs of malaria and is the standard remedy for chills and fever.

## RESORCIN

A compound preparation used locally for eczema and itching of the skin. It is also valuable in hay fever and whooping cough.

## RHUBARB

The root of a plant native to Asia and cultivated in America, preparations from which are used as a laxative. It increases the flow of bile, stimulates digestion and tones up the intestines. Its after effect is that of an astringent. It is often given with magnesia; sometimes also with calomel.

## ROCHELLE SALT

Tartrate of potassium and sodium. It is a gentle and cooling laxative. It is used in seidlitz powder.

## RUE

The root of the rue plant is of an irritating nature. In enemas it is used to remove intestinal worms and to check hysteria. It has a stimulating effect upon the nerves. It should be used with caution, as an overdose causes poisoning.

## SACCHARIN

A very sweet product of coal tar, being about two hundred times as sweet as cane sugar. It is used as a substitute for sugar in the food given for diabetes, as in this disease it is desirable to eliminate sugar and starch from the diet.

## SAFFRON

A plant, the flowers of which are used for medicinal purposes. It is a gastric and general stimulant. It is given sometimes to relieve flatulency. It is sometimes prescribed in cases of measles to stimulate eruption. Saffron is a powerful drug, and overdoses may cause stupor and even death.

## SALICYLIC ACID

The acid and its salts are used in the treatment of acute articular rheumatism, for gout and in ointments for the treatment of eczema, ulcers and wounds. Mixed with collodion, it is used to remove corns and warts.

## SARSAPARILLA

The root of this South American plant is used in various mixtures of medicines, but apparently has little or no curative value itself. It has been prescribed for gout, rheumatism and skin diseases, but its value, if any, consists in promoting the action of other drugs.

## SAVIN

A shrub resembling red cedar, the tops of which are used in the preparation of a medicine to relieve uterine hemorrhage. There is great danger in its use.

## SEIDLITZ POWDER

A compound effervescent powder, prepared in two parts, given as a cathartic. One part is composed of 120 grains of Rochelle salts and 40 grains bicarbonate of soda. The other part is 35 grains of tartaric acid. The first part is usually wrapped in blue paper, the second in white paper. Each is dissolved separately in water and then poured together, which causes effervescence, and in that condition it is drunk at once.

## SENNA

An African plant, preparations from which are given as purgatives. It is used in the compound powder of licorice as a laxative. Senna itself is rather harsh in its effects.

## SNAKEWEED

This plant, and other similar plants, including smartweed, are mild astringents. They are used internally and externally for relaxed conditions.

## SPERMACETI

An oily product of the sperm whale. In powder form, mixed with sugar, one part to three, it is taken for mild cases of sore throat and catarrhal inflammation of the air passages.

## STRYCHNINE

This is a poison. It is a valuable stimulant and tonic, and is also used in the treatment of lockjaw, epilepsy, neuralgia and constipation. There is always danger of poisoning in its use, and it should never be used except under the direction of a physician.

## SUGAR OF MILK

A sugar prepared from the whey of cow's milk. It is not as sweet as cane sugar, but is less apt to ferment, and so is better for sweetening infant's food. It is chiefly used as a vehicle for other medicines. It has a somewhat laxative effect. It increases the urine and is sometimes prescribed for dropsy.

## SULPHUR

This is a mineral substance which is used as a remedy for various skin diseases. It is applied in the form of ointment, and is especially effective in the treatment of itch. It is administered internally as a mild laxative. Solutions of sulphur in the form of various sulphur baths are supposed to be beneficial in cases of rheumatism and gout, as well as skin diseases.

## SULPHURIC ACID

This drug is a violent caustic and is destructive to any organic matter. It is used to remove warts, corns, to cauterize ulcers, and in diluted form is administered for the relief of different forms of diarrhea and cholera.

## SWEET SPIRITS OF NITER

A mixture of alcohol, water and ethyl nitrate. It acts upon the kidneys and the skin, producing a free flow of urine, and, when taken with hot water or lemonade, causes sweating. It is useful in the early stages of cold.

## TANNIC ACID

A yellowish white powder obtained from nutgall. It is one of the most common and effective astringents. Most vegetable astringents contain tannic acid. It is used to relieve diarrhea and dysentery, to check hemorrhages, also to toughen sensitive parts of the skin. Dissolved in water it is used for leucorrhea and similar unhealthy conditions of mucous membranes.

## TANSY

A common herb, preparations of which increase the flow of urine and other discharges. It is used to expel worms, for the relief of colic, and it is sometimes applied externally for bruises, sprains and muscular rheumatism. It contains a poisonous oil, and should be used with caution.

## TAR

A complex pitchy product of pine wood. It contains creosote. It is used in treating consumption and chronic bronchitis. In the form of oil of tar, diluted, it is used as a dressing for sores. In pills it is used for the relief of constipation.

## TARTARIC ACID

An acid common in many fruits, including grapes and pineapples. It is rarely used in medicine alone, but usually in combination with alkalies. It is one of the ingredients of seidlitz powder.

## TARTAR EMETIC

A preparation made from the metal antimony. It is a poisonous irritant which, in very small doses, stimulates the appetite and slightly stimulates the processes of assimilation; in larger doses, it causes relaxation of the muscles, dilating of blood vessels and perspiration. Its use in medicine is gradually being discontinued, but sometimes used as an emetic to relax muscular spasms in certain acute stages of bronchitis and pneumonia and croup. It depresses the heart action, and under no condition should it be given without advice of a physician.

## THOROUGHWORT

Also known as boneset. The leaves of the plant are used to make an infusion or tea that should be taken hot for the relief of chill and aching of the bones. In the grippe and malarial fever it increases the flow of urine, and is a mild cathartic. It is also taken to regulate impaired digestion and for tonic effects.

## THYMOL

It is derived from the oil of thyme, which is obtained from the thyme herb. It is used for the same antiseptic purposes as carbolic acid, but is not an irritant or a corrosive, and has an agreeable instead of an offensive odor. Its use is much to be preferred in surgery and medicine. It is applied to ulcers, suppurating wounds, and is an excellent antiseptic wash for nose, mouth and throat.

## TURPENTINE

The oil or spirits of turpentine is a fluid distilled from the exudations of the pine or fir tree. It is used as a counter irritant for the treatment of neuralgia and rheumatism. It is usually mixed with olive oil, chloroform or camphor in liniments. It is applied to the chest upon cloths wrung out of hot water for the relief of pneumonia, pleurisy and bronchitis, and to the abdomen for flatulency. It is also given internally and by enema in typhoid fever for the same complication.

## WHISKY

A distilled alcoholic liquor made from grain. Medicinally it is used most effectively with hot water. It is given in fainting, drowning and cases of exposure and exhaustion. When the pulse is rapid and weak it often helps to restore normal conditions.

## WILD CHERRY BARK

It is a bitter tonic, but chiefly used in the form of a syrup in the treatment of coughs. It tends to quiet the nerves in cases of bronchitis or throat irritation. It is mild in its effect, but has none of the harmful qualities of opiates used in many throat remedies.

## WINTERGREEN

The oil of wintergreen is a fluid obtained from the leaves of the checkerberry plant. It is applied locally to relieve articular rheumatism, neuralgia and other pains.

## WITCH-HAZEL

An extract made from the leaves and bark of the witch-hazel or hamamelis shrub. It contains tannic acid and is mildly astringent. It has a certain value in mild cases of sore throat. Internally, in the fluid extract, it is used for oozing from small veins, varicose ulcers, piles, and bleeding from the stomach and intestines. The solutions commonly used externally have their chief value in alcohol, witch-hazel itself having little or no value in the treatment of wounds, bruises and sprains, for which it is extensively used. Diluted alcohol is preferable, because not so expensive and just as effective for the purposes last named.

## VASELINE

A thick, oily product of petroleum. It is used as a lubricant upon the skin and mucous membranes, and as the base in the preparation of various ointments. Its chief value is to protect and lubricate; otherwise, it has little medicinal value.

## VERONAL

A complex crystallized powder used to cause sleep. It acts on the central nervous system.

## ZINC

The salts of this metal are used locally for various skin diseases, having an astringent and antiseptic effect. They are also used internally in the treatment of epilepsy, neuralgia and nervous conditions.

# DISEASES

**A** LIBERAL amount of space is devoted to this department in order to make it a fairly comprehensive dictionary of human ailments. The purpose is to describe, as far as possible, the nature and cause of each disease, the symptoms by which it may be identified, and, in general terms, what is regarded as the best treatment by the best physicians. The treatment indicated usually includes the care of the patient and remedies prescribed. We have not considered it wise nor safe to indicate doses in serious diseases. The physician should give such directions, and they should be carefully followed. The size of doses varies greatly for small children and grown people. There are so many things in the condition of the patient which may have a bearing upon the dose of a given medicine to be prescribed that only the trained physician can safely indicate the dose. In the more common diseases usually more detailed directions are given than in the rarer diseases.

## Diseases of Children

Considerable prominence is given to diseases of children. Many of these so-called children's diseases are sometimes contracted by adults, and many of the diseases not classed as children's diseases are among those from which children often suffer. Those usually classified as the diseases of childhood include the following: Chicken pox, cholera infantum, German measles, infantile paralysis, measles, meningitis, mumps, rickets, scarlet fever, whooping cough and worms. These will all be found in the regular alphabetical order of this department.

A careful study of the paragraphs devoted to the various diseases will not only broaden the general knowledge of things physical, but will teach one how to avoid and how to recognize diseases, and will warn against serious mistakes in the care of a patient, as well as teach the best things to do. The subject is so big and in its details so technical, that it would not be possible to treat each subject completely. We have simply tried to handle the matter in the way most comprehensive, practical and useful for a part of such a book as this.

## BACTERIA AND DISEASE

The remarkable progress of modern medical science is largely due to the discovery that most diseases are caused by germs. These minute organisms are best known as bacteria. They are the lowest form of life. Just as people may be classified as good and bad, so bacteria may be separated. We could not get along without bacteria. The beneficial forms render valuable service, and are found everywhere—in the air, the water, the earth and in most foods and drink.

### What Bacteria Do

The process of fermentation is accomplished by bacteria. Bacteria feed upon both living and dead organic matter, swarming in vegetable and animal organisms alike. Those found in dead organic matter accomplish the process of decomposition, and carry back to earth the elements to furnish food for plant life. All these activities are useful and necessary.

When bacteria appear in live animals or vegetables, and consume or poison the organic matter, they do harm in the sense of destroying life. These mischief makers include the bacteria or germs of disease.

## The Germ Theory of Disease

The bacteria, or germ theory of disease, has led scientists to hunt for the particular kind of bacteria that cause particular diseases. Their research and experiments have been rewarded with success in many instances. It has been possible to isolate and identify the bacteria of many diseases. Following up the discovery of the particular organisms that cause the disease, it has been possible to prove more positively how the germ gets into the body, its habits of growth, and to find out what can be used most successfully to kill the germ.

The experiments have brought out various drugs that are termed " specifics " in certain diseases, and which are practically certain to kill the germs of such diseases when brought in contact with them.

## Use of Antiseptics

One of the most important discoveries in this line is with reference to the use of antiseptics. As stated elsewhere, the remarkable achievements of modern surgery are due largely to cleanliness and the removal of all germs from the parts of the body under treatment. This is accomplished by thorough washing and the use of antiseptics. Any preparation that kills harmful bacteria and does not injure the body hastens recovery.

Another very important fact, which is receiving increasing attention from scientists, is that nature provides, within the body, ways and means of combating harmful bacteria. Were it not so, life would be impossible. Harmful bacteria are constantly passing through the body. So long as the health is good, and the various organs are doing their work vigorously, immunity against many diseases is maintained.

When any harmful bacteria gain a foothold in the system, certain changes occur in the fluids of the body and many of the most marked symptoms of disease are due to the attempts of nature to repel the invading and rapidly multiplying bacteria.

## Corpuscles and Bacteria in Battle

Scientists picturesquely describe the battles that take place in the body when bacteria come in conflict with the forces of the body that seek to destroy them. In the case of an infected wound, inflammation occurs through the attempts of the white blood corpuscles to combat the invading bacteria which are a rapidly multiplying army of destroyers. Breastworks are thrown up by the defenders for the protection of the surrounding tissues, and within this inclosure the combat rages.

Each army attempts the destruction of the other. Heat, redness, swelling and pain are the symptoms of this struggle. The result is a mass of pus made up of the dead bodies of the corpuscles mingled with overpowered bacteria and broken-down tissue.

## Toxines and Serum

In some diseases, toxines or poisons form in the body fluids that kill the diseased bacteria. The light-colored part of the blood, or serum, undergoes peculiar changes in many diseases. The change is permanent, apparently, in some diseases, thus establishing immunity. In such cases, a person who has had a certain disease will not contract it again. Following up the immunity theory, through investigation of serums, has led to the preparation of serums and anti-toxins that are administered to establish immunity against a certain disease, or to so modify the severity of an attack of the disease that recovery may be assured.

It was thus that the anti-toxin so successfully used in diphtheria came to be produced, and thus that serums have been made available for the treatment of hydrophobia, lockjaw, cerebro-spinal meningitis and several other diseases. Through the use of serum anti-toxins it is hoped to treat successfully the diseases that have hitherto been regarded as incurable, inasmuch as several such diseases have been conquered thus already. It is hoped also to make it possible to establish immunity against a considerable number of diseases by similar treatment to that of vaccination for smallpox.

Experiments are being conducted constantly with serums, and such progress has been made that it is believed possible thereby to successfully treat cancer, tuberculosis and other dreaded diseases. The discovery of the germ of leprosy has given assurance that it may be combated successfully by anti-toxin treatment.

## The Elusive Germ

So small are the bacteria of some diseases that it is difficult to discover them with even the most powerful microscopes. All efforts to find and identify the germs of measles and scarlet fever, for instance, have been unsuccessful. At the same time there seems to be no doubt that they are germ diseases.

A disease that has been especially baffling is cancer. Seemingly, by every possible method, attempts have been made to discover a germ cause of this disease, but nothing of the sort has yet been found.

## Prevention the Goal Sought

As soon as the germ of a particular disease is discovered, scientists feel, nowadays, that they have made great progress toward discovery of its prevention and cure. With the germ identified and isolated, experiments are conducted on animals, and serums are developed and tested until immunity is established, if possible. We are told, by those engaged in this work, that the hope for the race in its fight against disease rests in the future in serums and anti-toxins and preventive hygiene, and not in drugs.

## Antiseptics

Frequent reference is made throughout this book to the use of antiseptics, often without mentioning any particular antiseptic. Preparations that may be effective in destroying harmful bacteria are often of so poisonous a nature that they are dangerous for general home use. Antiseptics that may be applied to the body quite freely, with reasonable caution, include the following: Alcohol, dioxygen, peroxide of hydrogen, listerine and boracic acid. There are many more powerful antiseptics, but these are safe and effective for general purposes.

## ABDOMINAL PAINS

They may be due to a variety of causes in which any of the organs in that part of the body may be involved. If severe, and continue for a considerable time, a physician should be called to find out just what the disease is of which the pains are a symptom. There is liable to be great danger in such cases, if neglected. The best temporary treatment for abdominal pains is hot applications, which should be renewed as soon as they grow cool. Such applications may be poultices or hot water bottles, or hot enemas may be used.

## ABSCESS

A sore consisting of bacteria in the midst of broken-down tissue and blood corpuscles. External abscesses are usually due to infection which occurs by way of a hair or sweat gland, in which case they are called boils or carbuncles; when on the finger tips, felons. Abscesses occur in the internal organs due from some kind of infection, as, for instance, from tuberculosis, or from a diseased appendix. Abscesses of the brain sometimes result from infection through the middle ear; sometimes, also, after an injury.

The best treatment for abscesses that can be reached is to open them in their very earliest stages and apply antiseptics, to kill the bacteria that are making trouble. In every case absolute cleanliness should be maintained.

## ADENOIDS

A soft, spongy growth which often forms in the throats of children back of the nasal passages. They often interfere with breathing, and may cause deafness. The difficulty in breathing may lead to malformation of the chest and of the face, especially the nose, jaws and teeth. They may induce catarrh of the nose and throat, and may be a channel of infection for the germs of tuberculosis and other diseases. Adenoids should be removed by a surgeon.

## ALCOHOLISM

The repeated and excessive use of alcoholic drink leads to poisoning of the system, and the various organs are not able to perform their normal functions. Permanent and positively serious effects follow habitual intoxication. Treatment involves the practice of total abstinence, the patient being gradually brought to that point. The system must be built up and the poison gradually driven out through the habits of simple, nutritious diet, exercise, plenty of sleep, good air and frequent bathing. Drug treatments for the alcohol habit are either ineffective or dangerous.

## ANAEMIA

This is a condition of the blood due to a lack of hæmoglobin, or the iron constituents of the blood.

One of the noticeable symptoms is extreme pallor of skin and mucous membranes. Red cells of the blood, which give it the characteristic color, absorb and retain oxygen supplied to the body through the lungs. The better the service of supplying oxygen is performed the more healthy will be the tissues of the body. In cases of anæmia the blood is lacking in essential elements, including albumen and salts. The watery part of the blood may be increased so that there is as much in quantity, but it is not good blood. The result is a weakened condition of the entire body.

The cause may be insufficient nourishment, dark and damp living quarters, extremes of heat or cold in the place where one habitually stays, lack of sleep and sometimes minor disorders. The use of extremely tight corsets is sometimes said to cause anæmia because the vital organs are so compressed that they are unable to properly do their work.

In treating the disorder it is important to discover the cause and remove it. The surroundings of the patient should be made as good as possible and through correct habits and nourishing diet the system should be built up if possible. There is danger in overfeeding with rich food, for this will cause further impairment of the digestive organs.

The desire of the patient for salty or acid foods may be gratified, but an abnormal craving for indigestible things should be denied, as they would only irritate the stomach.

## ANTHRAX

A blood disease that is usually fatal in man. It is transmitted from some animal; cattle, horses, sheep, hogs and goats being addicted to it. It may be taken by handling the skin or wool of an animal that has had the disease. The anthrax germ may enter the skin through a small wound. There is a rapidly developing inflammation, followed by a forming of a vesicle, which breaks, and a dark crust forms. This is surrounded by inflamed swelling and bluish discoloration. Generally infection develops with a fever, although the fever is sometimes absent; in severe cases headaches, pains in the limbs, weakness, difficulty in breathing, vomiting, diarrhea, hemorrhages and stupor follow infection. If infection comes through breathing dust, symptoms resembling pneumonia develop. Sometimes infection is conveyed with the food to the stomach and intestines, causing severe intestinal pains, with vomiting and diarrhea.

The disease develops rapidly and no special treatment except by surgical operation has been established. Serum is used in the treatment of cattle suffering from anthrax, and it is expected that the most successful treatment of man will be found to be with similar serum.

## APPENDICITIS

The appendix is a wormlike attachment to the beginning of the large intestine, having no known use. The form and position of the organ make it an easy victim to bacterial infection. There are all grades of inflammation, from a simple chronic congestion, causing slight digestive disturbances, to the acute gangrenous form which may cause death in a few days. The symptoms of an acute attack are pain in the abdomen, nausea, vomiting and constipation, and tenderness and rigidity over the right lower part of the abdomen. The only safe treatment is early operation.

## APOPLEXY

Apoplexy is a plugging or bursting of a blood vessel of the brain, usually occurring in advanced life. A blood clot formed in one of the big arteries of the body is sometimes carried into the blood vessels of the brain and lodges there, causing the trouble. Usually an apoplectic stroke takes place after some unusual excitement or after a hearty meal or excessive drinking. There is a rush of blood to the head and a rupture of the blood vessel results. Then comes the pressure upon the brain, with resulting paralysis, usually on one side only, and a softening of the brain substance results.

If the hemorrhage of the brain is profuse a vital part is usually affected and death occurs. More frequently the blood is absorbed, but the brain is left with a scar and a measure of one-sided paralysis continues; but only a small part of the body is sometimes affected. The mind of the patient may or may not be noticeably injured. There is always danger of recurrent strokes with increasing danger of fatal results.

Preventive treatment consists of correct habits and avoiding causes which might result in congestion of blood to the head. Very little can be done after an apoplectic stroke. The patient should be put to bed, with the head and shoulders raised. Cold applications should be applied to the head and heat to the feet. The bowels should be moved with an enema and a light liquid diet should be given. No stimulants should be administered.

## ASTHMA

Asthma is a disease of the respiratory organs, due to a spasmodic contraction of the smaller bronchial tubes, causing great difficulty of breathing, with wheezing and a suffocating sensation. It is usually of nervous origin and lasts but a few hours. In some cases the condition persists for days and even weeks, with alternating periods of improvement. If the disease is caused by chronic catarrh or some growth and enlargement in the throat or nose, as is sometimes the case, it may be cured by proper treatment of the difficulties that cause it.

Among the remedies used for asthma are mustard plasters applied to the chest; putting the hands or feet in hot water; smoking sage tobacco and other plant leaves, and inhaling fumes of burning paper soaked with a mild solution of saltpeter. The use of so-called asthma cures that are advertised do little or no good, and often much harm. The cure is really accomplished by getting the patient into as good a condition of vigorous health as possible; plenty of outdoor exercise that is not too vigorous, regular habits of sleep, and avoiding extreme fatigue help to bring about the desired result.

## ASPHYXIA

This is a state of unconsciousness due to lack of oxygen in the blood and the term is applied usually to cases where this condition is caused suddenly. For instance, through inhaling poisonous gas; by drawing food into the windpipe, the result of which we call choking; drowning; pleurisy, which causes undue pressure upon the lungs; and in pneumonia. Asphyxia may be caused by taking large doses of certain drugs, especially headache powders. The danger from the latter comes from acetanilid, which is found in most headache powders. Acute alcoholism or opium poison may develop asphyxia. The patient becomes unconscious, with a bluish appearance of the skin and especially lips, and has blood-shot eyes. Where the aggravating cause may be removed, it should be removed as soon as possible. This should be followed by vigorous rubbing and stimulants and artificial respiration.

## BARBER'S ITCH

This is a skin disease of the bearded part of the .ace, in which red and inflamed spots, with pustules that lead to the root of the hair, appear. As the disease continues, crusts form upon the skin; the hairs become brittle and fall out, and the disease defies any mild healing treatment. It is caused by a microscopic form of fungus which attacks the hair shaft and follicle.

In its earliest stages, treatment should be thorough, washing with pure soap, the extraction of the hairs involved, application of mild antiseptic solutions. If the disease spreads, treatment should be under the direction of a physician.

## BILIOUSNESS

This is a sort of blood poisoning or toxemia, manifested by loss of appetite, badly coated tongue, foul taste in the mouth on arising, headache, constipation, sleepiness and general ill-feeling, and sometimes slight jaundice. The liver and its ducts may become swollen, and the bile cease to flow freely into the intestines. The lack of bile causes fermentation and putrefaction in the intestines, and sometimes catarrhal inflammation of the stomach, with nausea and vomiting.

The disease is caused by excessive eating, particularly of foods that include much sweets and fats, lack of exercise and alcoholic drinking.

The treatment should be very simple diet—perhaps taking only water for a time, in acute cases—mild cathartics and hot water enemas.

## BLADDER DISEASES

Inflammation of the bladder is always due to some infection that attacks the lining membrane, the exciting cause of which may be an irritation from gravel or stones, formed by the gathering of deposits upon some particles that find their way into the urinary tract, or excited by exposure to cold, or injuries to the lining of the organ by blows or falls. Infection is caused by retention of urine, due to the narrowing or obstruction of the passage by stricture, or an enlargement of the prostate gland. Tuberculosis, kidney disease or an inflammation of the urinary passage may cause it. The symptoms include pain and difficulty in passing urine, and a constant desire to urinate.

Treatment should include complete rest and quiet, securing steady bodily warmth, warm baths and simple food. Avoid the so-called hard or mineral waters. A surgical operation may be necessary to secure relief.

## BLOOD POISONING

The poisoning of the whole system caused by certain bacteria absorbed through the circulation of the blood. It may originate from a variety of causes, notably from a wound which has not received proper care as to absolute cleanliness. The symptoms include chills, high temperature, weakness and in certain cases unconsciousness. The only way to avoid these dangerous conditions is by prompt treatment of every injury and inflammation where pus is present.

There should be proper incisions made and antiseptic applications to prevent the distribution of bacteria and absorption by the blood of so-called toxic matter. Treatment of serious cases of blood poisoning can only be accomplished safely by direction of a physician. The bowels should be kept open and the patient should be given plenty of water and all the salt solution that can be absorbed by the rectum. Stimulants and quietening medicines are given if they become necessary.

## BOIL

A boil is an abscess that forms in the skin and is due usually to the entrance of an infection through a pore of the skin or by a slight injury. The theory that a boil is an effort on the part of nature to throw off impurities is incorrect. Persons run down, or with poor blood, may suffer from boils, but they are not benefited by them, nor the blood improved. The old-fashioned method of poulticing a boil as soon as it begins to form has the effect of encouraging the multiplication of disease germs. The germs multiply much more rapidly by the application of heat.

Proper treatment is to make a free opening with a sharp, pointed knife that has been soaked in some antiseptic solution, after which an antiseptic poultice should be applied. This is made by dipping a piece of gauze in a boracic acid solution, applying it as hot as it can be borne. There is danger in massaging or squeezing a boil, as the poisonous matter is liable to be worked through the protecting formation that nature provides and sent into the system, causing more or less serious blood poisoning. A person who is subject to boils should avoid starchy foods, constipation should be guarded against, also excessive exercise or too frequent bathing.

### Carbuncle

Carbuncles are also a kind of abscess, but form deeper below the surface, and are more extensive, more powerful and more dangerous than boils. They discharge by several openings. The treatment is similar to that for boils. It is best to have them lanced early by a surgeon and antiseptic treatment applied.

### BRIGHT'S DISEASE

A variety of kidney diseases are brought under this term. They are characterized by inflammation, which usually starts in the kidneys themselves, but may begin in any portion of the urinary canal and extend to the kidneys. The powers of the kidneys are impaired and they are unable to throw off the waste matter of the system as they should. A large amount of albumen escapes from the blood with the urine. Dropsy may develop, also uremia, which is systematic poisoning from the absorption of waste products. Bright's disease is often brought on by exposure to wet and cold; from various infectious diseases; from the excessive use of alcohol, and from poisonous drugs.

The symptoms of acute Bright's disease include

headache, scanty and high-colored urine, some disturbances of the stomach. Loss of flesh and strength follow, and dropsy sets in. In many cases uremia develops. There may be shortness of breath and a weak or rapid pulse. There may be a complete recovery after several weeks or months, or the disease may terminate fatally in a short time.

In chronic Bright's disease similar symptoms appear in less marked degree, coming on slowly. There may be at first an increase in the amount of urine, especially at night, which is followed later by a decrease and the ordinary symptoms of the acute form. The disease may last ten or fifteen years. Many afflicted with it die of apoplexy, many from other disorders which arise and many also recover.

A milk diet often gives good results. The extensive use of meats and stimulants should be avoided. Frequent warm baths and a special friction to prevent chilling of the body are recommended. Bodily and mental rest are desirable, as well as careful regulation of the diet.

## BRONCHITIS

This is an inflammation of the mucous membranes of the bronchial tubes. It may involve one or both sides and affect only the larger tubes or the entire so-called bronchial tree. It is a form of acute catarrh, caused by colds usually, and may be due to inhaling gas, smoke or dust. Poisonous gases are especially dangerous. Acute bronchitis may begin with fever quite suddenly, and sometimes with a chill. Often, however, there is no fever. The most notable symptoms are cough and raising of mucus from the throat. The sensation of tickling and soreness in the throat, and soreness behind the upper part of the breast bone, is constantly felt.

There is danger, especially in children and old people, of the inflammation involving the lungs, and this is known as broncho-pneumonia. The inflammation then endangers life. In the milder forms of bronchitis or bronchial catarrh, it gradually disappears within a week or two. If fever develops, the patient should go to bed and a physician should be called immediately.

Cases of chronic bronchitis may be due to repeated attacks of the acute form, but more often to a diseased condition of the heart or some other internal organ, which causes a chronic congestion of the pulmonary vessels. An obstinate cough is among the symptoms. Recovery should be sought by avoiding irritants, such as dust, smoke and alcohol. Complete bodily rest should be sought.

The first step toward recovery is the removal of the cause, and study should, therefore, be made of the disease back of the bronchitis. This calls for the services of a good physician.

## BRUISES

Injuries caused by a blow or fall cause more or less crushing of the muscles, and usually break some of the smaller blood vessels. The less serious should be treated with cold applications and pressure. Diluted alcohol, arnica, witch-hazel extract or a solution of sugar of lead, alum and water may be used. If the skin is cold, cold applications should not be used, but the injury should be bathed with an antiseptic and bandaged. Massage is frequently advisable to facilitate the absorption of blood forced into the tissues through ruptured veins.

For bruises in which the skin is broken, the same treatment is required as for other wounds, to guard against infection of bacteria.

## BUNION

A deformity of the great toe caused by wearing narrow-pointed shoes. There is a displacement of the joint where the toe joins the foot proper. The bones are enlarged and the ligaments of the joint are thickened. Inflammation and pain often occur, If an abscess forms, it should be opened. Broad-toed shoes should be worn. Sometimes conditions are improved by wearing some contrivance to force the great toe back toward its natural position. Bunions are prevented by wearing comfortable, well-fitting shoes that do not crowd the toes.

## BUBONIC PLAGUE

This disease, in epidemic form, known simply as the plague, has swept away millions of people in eastern countries. Many years ago it frequently spread through Europe, where it was known as the "Black Death." It is a germ disease, which is carried from one person to another, but is more often carried by animals, especially rats. There is most danger of it in dark, dirty, unhealthful buildings.

The germ gains entrance to the body through the respiratory system, the digestive tract and broken-down skin surfaces. The disease develops rapidly with high temperature, delirium, hemorrhages and enlarged and often suppurating glands or buboes, from which the disease takes its name.

The patient should be kept strictly isolated, and absolute cleanliness is necessary. As a preventive measure, rats should be kept exterminated so far as possible, and cleanliness of person and surroundings should be maintained.

## CANCER

A malignant form of tumor, no cure for which has yet been discovered. The exact cause of the disease is not yet known. Many things have been discovered about cancer in recent years, which it is expected will lead to the discovery of some method of cure or immunity. Apparently, cancer is not caused by any germ, either bacterial or parasitic, but spreads through the growth of its own peculiar cells, which take the place of the natural cells of the body.

It has been found that a person who has recovered from a cancer is thereafter immune. Recoveries, which are rare, have never resulted from any particular treatment apparently, but have occurred because of some agency within the body itself. Cancers are usually removed by cutting, but sometimes successfully by the use of a caustic. Cancers spread through the blood and lymph vessels, and the sooner they are removed, the more chance there is of complete recovery.

Some of the more dangerous forms of cancer are those of the internal organs. Cancer of the liver is considered fatal, and cancer of the stomach is attended by great danger; also cancerous troubles of the abdominal organs, but cures are sometimes effected by operations. No reliance should be placed upon the frequently advertised cures for cancer without the use of the knife.

## CANKER

Canker in the mouth appears in nursing and bottle-fed babies, and is caused by the growth of a vegetable fungus resembling the yeast plant on the mucous membrane. It appears as white spots, surrounded by a narrow, inflamed strip. The mouth should be washed out after each feeding with a solution of boracic acid as strong as can be made. Cover the finger with a piece of absorbent cotton, dip it into the solution and swab the mouth thoroughly.

## CHICKEN POX

Chicken pox is an acute contagious disease of childhood. It comes on about twelve days after exposure, often beginning with a slight chill and fever, which is followed in about twenty-four hours by the presence on the body of a number of raised red papules, which, in a few hours more, are filled with the clear or milky fluid which changes later to pus. By the end of the week, the pustules are dried into brown crusts. Fresh crops of these papules appear during the first few days, so that papules, vesicles and pustules may all be present at the same time. This is never the case in smallpox.

Although chicken pox resembles a mild case of smallpox, it is an entirely different disease, and one does not protect against the other. There is much itching of the skin, but scratching should be avoided, as it causes ulcers and scars.

The skin should be bathed occasionally in a soda or weak carbolic acid solution, ten drops of a mixture of glycerin and carbolic acid to a large wash basin of warm water. In order to prevent spread of the disease, the patient should be isolated, and one should make sure that the disease really is chicken pox and not smallpox.

## CHILBLAINS

These are swellings caused by paralysis and dilation of the blood vessels after they have been disturbed by severe cold. They appear upon the toes, fingers, ears and nose. Although usually caused by exposure when the temperature is below freezing, they may also result from frequent washing in cold water. Chilblains may be prevented by encouraging the circulation of blood in the hands and feet.

The treatment may include bathing in hot water, with a few drops of ammonia added. Tincture of iodine may help, if painted upon the surface. Among the remedies prescribed are equal parts of castor oil and balsam of Peru; or apply a coating of a preparation consisting of tannic acid two drams, carbolic acid twenty-four drops, alcohol four drams and water enough to make an ounce in all. Apply with a brush night and morning.

## CHOLERA

Asiatic cholera is an infectious disease caused by germs taken into the body with contaminated drinking water. The germ of cholera was discovered by Robert Koch. It gains access to the intestines and multiplies very rapidly, producing poisonous substances that are absorbed and cause diseased conditions in various parts of the body. The early symptoms are usually nausea, restlessness and chilly sensations, followed by violent and frequently recurring diarrhea and vomiting. Then, there is dizziness, palpitation of the heart, a gray appearance to the face and blueness of the body. Pain in the stomach and region of the heart is often severe. There are cramps in the calves and arms.

The patient suffers continually from thirst. Urine may be suppressed. The patient sinks into unconsciousness, and in that condition may die. Otherwise, he may suddenly improve and then either recover or sink into a fatal state of unconsciousness which terminates in a few days.

There is so much danger of spreading the disease that great care should be taken in disposing of all waste matter from the patient. There is no dependable remedy for cholera, and treatment should be entirely under the direction of a physician.

Among the preparations prescribed is a mixture of one part each of rhubarb, spirits of peppermint, camphor, capsicum and opium. From ten to twenty drops in a glass of water is the dose prescribed. Hoffmann's anodyne is also prescribed. This consists of four ounces of ether, eight ounces of alcohol and 150 minims of ethereal oil. From twenty to sixty drops are given as a dose.

## CHOLERA INFANTUM

This disease attacks children during the summer months. It is a violent inflammation of the stomach and bowels. Germs in milk usually cause the trouble. The attack comes on suddenly, with severe vomiting and purging; pain in the abdomen, which becomes distended and sensitive, high fever, feeble pulse and coldness of the surface, with muscular spasms and often general convulsions. A physician should be summoned immediately. No nourishment should be given, and thirst should be satisfied with boiled water until further directions are given by the physician.

## CHOLERA MORBUS

Cholera morbus is an inflammation of the stomach and intestines, the cause of which is usually decomposition of food, as the result of heat in the summer. Another cause is sometimes the drinking of too much very cold beverages when the body is overheated. The disease appears with acute pain in the abdomen, nausea, vomiting, watery diarrhea, cramps in the legs and cold, clammy skin.

The patient should be kept quiet in bed, and there should be continual applications of heat to the abdomen. This should be dry; hot water bottles, hot sand bags or similar things may be used. The first treatment should be the giving of a cathartic; castor oil, for instance. Hot water only should be given internally. It is well to abstain from food for at least twelve or twenty-four hours.

## COLDS

A cold is a contagious disease, due to the entrance through the respiratory tract of some organism which attacks, primarily, the mucous membrane, usually beginning with the nose and throat. It attacks most often those living in poorly ventilated dwellings and among bad hygienic surroundings, and those of lowered vitality. Colds are unknown among Arctic explorers while on their expeditions.

Frequently repeated colds by those who still retain the germs may be brought on by chilling of the surface of the body, which drives the blood from the surface, causing a congestion in the internal organs. Any organ that has been weakened will be the first to suffer, and will become the seat of congestion. Bacteria multiply in the weakened organ and cause the various disorders that appear with a cold.

Colds may be prevented by keeping the skin healthy and well nourished, so that being rich in blood it is capable of reacting when exposed to low temperature. The first treatment for a cold should be to bring about profuse perspiration, stimulating the blood vessels of the skin. This may be done by hot baths, hot applications in the form of packs, and administering hot beverages. The object to be attained is a readjustment of the circulation of the blood in the various organs of the body.

## COLIC

This is a condition of acute pain caused by spasmodic contraction of the muscles of the internal organs. It usually occurs in the intestine. Because of the presence of undigested food, fermentation and inflammation gases contribute chiefly to the disturbance. Colic is a symptom rather than a disease, and may indicate some simple irritation or presence of a tumor or adhesions of the intestine.

The treatment should be hot applications over the site of the pain, and hot baths sometimes give relief. Hot water or soap enemas sometimes relieve colic pains in the intestine. When the acute pains have been relieved the cause of the trouble should be discovered and receive treatment.

## CONCUSSION OF THE BRAIN

A severe blow on the head often so disturbs the brain as to cause unconsciousness and lack of sensation. A low pulse, weak breathing and vomiting follow. There is often danger that there may be a fracture of the skull in addition to the concussion of the brain. The person injured should be moved very carefully, all clothing should be loosened and his head placed low.

If able to swallow, he should be given water. Never attempt artificial respiration. Further treatment should be under the direction of a physician. The patient must be kept very quiet.

## CONSTIPATION

This disorder is usually due to either the wrong kind of diet or unhealthy habits of living. It is important that the diet consist of a liberal quantity of bulky and juicy foods. The intestine requires the stimulation which a fresh vegetable diet gives. Such concentrated food as meat causes less contraction for the walls of the intestines, and their muscles become weakened. A lack of exercise tends to this condition. Tight lacing has been the cause of this disorder with many girls and women.

Walking and special exercises which employ muscles of the abdomen help to ward off constipation. The treatment should include a careful diet, consisting in a general way of the coarse breads and cereals, cream, fresh, juicy fruits and vegetables and juicy meats; and drinking large quantities of water. Foods to be especially avoided are white bread, baked beans, pork, veal, eggs and any kind of salted, dried or preserved meats, nuts, cheese, milk and tea.

One should take a glass of cold water before breakfast and before retiring. There should be careful massage of the abdomen, and prompt and regular attention to the movements of the bowels. In the more serious cases, enemas of water or oil may be given. Cathartics should be avoided, as they overstimulate the intestines, leaving them more sluggish afterwards.

Among the fruits specially recommended are grapes, which may be eaten in liberal quantities. The patient should eat freely, having in mind the fact that the intestinal muscles are to be stimulated by food in which protein is not prominent.

## CONSUMPTION

Tuberculosis of the lungs. This is a very common and very fatal disease. It may appear in the acute form, which runs to a fatal conclusion within a few weeks, or in the chronic form, which may last for several years. It is infectious, and is caused by a germ that enters the body and forms in the lungs a large number of tubercles—little gray bodies about the size of a pin head. The tubes and walls of the lungs become more or less filled with the tubercles, and, as the disease develops, there is a breaking down of the lung tissues, the progress of the disease being destructive.

The early symptoms include a dry, teasing cough, loss of strength and flesh, a rapid pulse, and a slight rise of temperature in the afternoon. Some-

times the first symptom noticed is a sudden
hemorrhage. The patient steadily loses strength
and the coughing increases and becomes more distressing, with more and more expectoration, which
becomes thicker and yellow in color. Sometimes
there is pain in the chest, and the general debility
that attends the disease may lead to complication
of other organs, including digestive troubles, kidney and heart disease.

## Danger from Infection

As the disease is infectious, great care should be
taken to avoid it. It is important to maintain
good sanitary conditions and seek sunlight and
fresh air, remembering also that only under conditions of lowered vitality is one likely to acquire
consumption. The disease is not hereditary, except in very rare instances, but there may be a
hereditary tendency to acquire the disease; and in
all cases where the health is not vigorous or the
sanitary conditions surrounding one are not good,
there is always danger.

The germs of the disease are expectorated by
those afflicted, and, becoming dried, are breathed in
with the dust, or enter the stomach upon articles
of food, and then pass into the circulation.

## Air and Nutrition

Consumption in its early stages is cured by a
course of treatment which includes rest, living and
sleeping in the open air, cold baths and an abundance of nourishing food—the one purpose being to
make the general health and store of physical vitality as great as possible. This means the death of
the germ in the early stages of consumption.

As people have come to realize more keenly the conditions under which consumption flourishes, and the conditions under which it cannot exist, the death rate from the disease has rapidly decreased, and more and more attention is given to sanitary environment, and the avoidance of infection from those suffering with the disease.

Tuberculosis is not always confined to the lungs, but may develop in other parts of the body, including bones, skin and bowels.

## CONVULSIONS

Convulsions are violent, spasmodic, muscular contractions, accompanied by unconsciousness. They are not a disease, but a symptom of some disease or brain irritation. They are most common in infancy. Among the most frequent causes in children are some digestive disturbance, meningitis or the onset of some contagious disease. Teething, which is so often assigned as the cause of infantile convulsions, is almost never the cause of that or any other serious condition.

The attacks usually appear suddenly, the face becoming pale, the eyes fixed or rolled upward, consciousness is lost, and there are spasmodic twitchings of the face and extremities, followed by a retraction of the head and clenching of the hands, and violent contractions of all the muscles. The respirations are shallow, and the face becomes blue and distorted. One attack is very apt to be followed by others. Death from convulsions is generally due to exhaustion from rapidly recurring attacks.

## For a Child

If the patient is a child, place it in a warm bath with a cold sponge on the head, and move bowels by enema, and, after the attack, keep it as quiet as possible, to avoid a fresh outburst. The treatment for adults should include loosening the clothing about the neck and chest, placing a wedge between the jaws, if possible, to prevent injury to the tongue. Give plenty of air.

Convulsions call for the presence of a physician, especially because of the fact that they are symptoms of serious trouble requiring expert attention.

## CORNS

Corns consist of thickening and hardening of part of the skin, usually over the little toe. Hard layers of skin form and, instead of being like other callouses, a sort of plug presses down upon the nerves below the skin, which is very sensitive.

The treatment consists in removal of the thickened skin or hard plug in the skin which constitutes the corn. This may be done by scraping off the layers with a sharp knife, using great care if bleeding is caused, to avoid infection. Before any attempt is made to remove the corn, it should be loosened by some application. For instance, a 50 per cent solution of potash lye.

The removal of the corn may be accomplished by the use of a caustic. A saturated solution of salicylic acid in collodion may be applied. It acts slowly, but is not painful, and accomplishes the desired result.

Corns are caused by tight or ill-fitting shoes, and great care should be used in selecting shoes that are comfortable.

## CROUP

Croup is a catarrhal spasm of the larynx, usually occurring in children under the age of five. It is most frequently associated with enlarged tonsils and adenoid growths. The exciting cause may be exposure to cold, or an attack of indigestion, and the inflammation of the larynx is added and spasmodic contraction of the vocal chord, causing a narrowing of the opening, preventing the entrance of air. The attack may come on without warning, or be preceded for several hours by hoarseness and a barking cough, which grows worse about midnight, with difficulty in breathing. The child wakes suddenly, terrified, sits up in bed, struggles for breath, inspiration is difficult, prolonged and crowing. The cough is hoarse, barking and metallic.

The symptoms are most alarming to the uninitiated, and out of all proportion to the seriousness of the disease itself. The attack gradually wears away, and in an hour or so the child falls asleep, and the next day only a slight cough and hoarseness remain. But if left to itself, the attack is likely to be repeated on the next two nights, after which the child is as well as usual until change in weather or diet precipitates another attack.

The purpose of treatment during the spasm is to produce relaxation of the contracting muscles. This is accomplished by hot, moist compressions to the throat and inhalations of steam. If necessary, half a teaspoonful of ipecac may be given to induce vomiting. As a preventive, fresh air, cold sponging and the removal of any adenoid growths or enlarged tonsils are recommended.

So-called membranous croup is a form of diphtheria.

## DANDRUFF

A disturbance of the oil glands of the scalp, causing an excessive dryness and the formation of scales which come off freely. It is usually confined to the top and crown of the head. The hairs, deprived of the necessary lubricant, become dry and fall out, and if the condition is not soon arrested, baldness results. The hair and scalp should be kept clean by washing with castile soap and warm water. All soap should be washed away, the hair gently dried and the following formula rubbed into the scalp: Mix 2½ parts each of resorcin and castor oil in 20 parts of cologne water, adding enough alcohol to make 100 parts. This treatment should be repeated two or three times a week.

In order to keep the hair in good condition, cleanliness is important, but washing should not occur any oftener than is necessary for cleanliness, and strong soap should be avoided. The condition of the hair depends, to quite a degree, on the oil in it. Too much washing and the use of harsh soap removes the oil and leaves the hair and scalp unnaturally dry. Frequent massage of the scalp with the finger tips, brushing the hair with a good bristle brush, but never with a metal brush, stimulate the health of the scalp and hair and promote hair growth.

### Baldness Cure

Kerosene oil is perhaps the best cure for approaching baldness. It is best applied by putting the oil in a little oiler like that used for bicycles, sewing machines and typewriters and placing the end of the oiler close to the scalp, leaving a drop in a space, taking care not to wet the hair with the oil more than is necessary. It spreads widely and rapidly over the surface. This should be applied upon going to bed, once a month only. In the morning if the hair is shaken out and exposed to the sunshine and air for a few minutes the odor of the oil will disappear. After the hair has fallen out to the extent of baldness there is little hope of its growing again. All hair dyes are more or less harmful and should not be used.

## DEAFNESS

The ear is an exceedingly complicated and delicate organ. The external ear is a shell-like cartilaginous structure for collecting the sound waves. It leads into a canal about 1½ inches long, known as the external auditory canal. A membrane, known as the ear drum or tympanic membrane, is stretched across the inner end. This separates the external from the middle ear. The sound waves passing through the external into the middle ear cause the tympanic membrane to vibrate and this produces a movement of the delicate ear bones that stretch across the cavity of the middle ear. This impulse is transmitted through another membrane to the internal ear, a bony labyrinth containing a liquid which is set into vibration by these sound waves and plays upon the delicate nerve endings arranged like the keys of a piano.

The sense of hearing is impaired to a greater or lesser degree by any injury or disease of the auditory apparatus, blows upon the head or loud, explosive sounds. Large masses of wax may collect in the canal, however, and press upon the drum, causing more or less pain, ringing in the ear and deafness.

A catarrhal inflammation causing a closure of the tube leading from the middle ear to the throat also produces similar symptoms.

## Abscess of Middle Ear

The most serious conditions are those due to infection and the formation of abscess in the middle ear. This may come on independently, but often follows certain diseases such as grippe, measles, scarlet fever, pneumonia or smallpox.

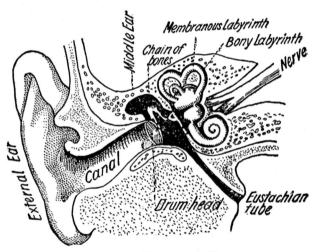

SECTIONAL VIEW OF THE EAR

The treatment is early incision of the drum, permitting free drainage of the abscess. It should be frequently syringed with a boracic acid solution and dried with sterile cotton. The use of oil in the ear should be avoided, as it tends to multiply bacteria and increase infection. If these cases are neglected the destruction of the middle ear and its surrounding bony walls, and even perforation into the brain itself, may result.

Hereditary deafness involves some defect in the nerve of hearing. This class of cases are less likely to be benefited by treatment.

Ear trumpets are usually unsatisfactory, but anyone having defective hearing will do well to experiment with some of the different kinds. The numerous devices advertised as overcoming all defects of hearing are almost invariably frauds. It is best to follow the directions of a physician in this matter.

## DIABETES

Diabetes is a disease in which a form of sugar called glucose is passed in the urine, instead of being assimilated by digestion as it should be. It is not a disease of the kidneys, but of some of the other organs, as the pancreas, liver or possibly of the nervous system itself. There is an increase in the amount of urine; there is loss of flesh and strength and an abnormal appetite and thirst. The disease may prove fatal within a few months, usually so with children, or may last for many years.

The symptoms usually include nervousness, difficulty in sleeping and some headache. As the disease progresses, the amount of urine increases to a very large amount. The sugar excreted may be in excess of that taken in food. The patient grows more emaciated, sometimes consumption develops and sometimes acute pneumonia. Boils and carbuncles frequently appear, and are dangerous, because the diabetic condition is liable to cause fatal blood poisoning from them.

Treatment should include, among other things, a diet which largely restricts foods yielding sugar in the process of digestion. This includes the starchy foods. Fruits should be eaten freely, especially acid fruits. The patient should have plenty of rest, exercise, fresh air, baths, and so regulate his habits as to improve his general physical condition to the highest possible degree.

## DIPHTHERIA

This is an infectious disease caused by a germ that induces inflammation of the mucous membrane of the throat, nose and mouth. What is known as a false membrane forms, having a gray color. It appears upon the tonsils first, usually, and spreads to the soft palate. Aside from the inflammation of the membrane, the disease affects the general system, according to the degree which the poisons produced locally are absorbed.

Sometimes diphtheria attacks the larynx and trachea, and is sometimes known as membranous croup, which is very dangerous, and tends to obstruct the air passages. The symptoms of the disease vary, according to the severity. They may include chills, fever, nausea, vomiting, headache, difficulty in swallowing, pains in the throat, and hoarseness. Gray patches appear in the throat and the tonsils are red and swollen. There is painful swelling of the glands in the neck.

In mild cases the symptoms pass away in a few days; in more severe cases the symptoms grow worse; there is general weakness and the poisoning of the system causes a weakened condition of the heart, lungs, kidneys and nerves. Death may be caused by interference with breathing, heart failure or paralysis.

The treatment should include the injection of anti-toxin serum at the earliest opportunity, absolute cleanliness, free use of dioxygen and boracic acid solutions or other antiseptics for sprays and gargles. Cold applications applied to the throat are recommended. Careful attention should be given to the possibility of restricted breathing or choking. This requires the attention of a physician.

Good air should be provided freely, without drafts, and the patient should be kept in strict quarantine, and careful disinfecting of everything used in the care of the patient.

## DROWNING

Drowning causes death in either of two ways—by shock or by suffocation. The appearance of the victim, if suffering from shock, is one of pallor, while suffocation, as in all cases of asphyxia, causes the appearance of lividity. In one case the face is white and the other red. These indications are signs of death, if the victim is unconscious and has stopped breathing; but in many cases it is possible to revive the victim by persistent effort, and in every case such effort should be made. There have been cases where the efforts of hours spent upon those apparently drowned have finally resulted in recovery.

To revive from drowning the first essentials are the restoration of breathing and body heat, and the maintenance of the latter. Remember that every moment is precious. Loosen or cut apart all neck bands so as to remove obstructions to breathing. Warmed blankets should be wrapped around the body and hot water bottles or hot bricks applied. At the same time turn the patient on his face, with head lower than body, grasping body about the middle and raising as far as you can without lifting the head off the ground; give the body a sharp jerk to remove mucus from throat and water from windpipe. ˙ Holding the body suspended, slowly count 1, 2, 3, and then repeat the jerk gently two or three times.

## Artificial Respiration

Place body on ground again, face downward; stand astride the body, holding it by the joints of the shoulders. Raise the chest as far as possible without lifting the head from the ground; hold it long enough to slowly count three. Replace the body on the ground with forehead resting on the arm that has been bent at the elbow. Be sure that nose and mouth are free, so that they can take in air.

With elbows against knees for a leverage, press downward and inward with increasing force against the side of the victim's chest and over the lower ribs long enough to count two, then let go suddenly. Grasp the shoulders as before and raise the chest, remembering to leave the forehead resting on the ground. Replace the body on the ground, pressing downward and inward against the sides of the chest, let go suddenly and, grasping the shoulders, raise the chest and press upon the ribs. If necessary, repeat these alternate movements for an hour at least at the rate of fifteen times a minute unless breathing is restored sooner.

Don't get discouraged. Work persistently. People have been restored to consciousness by persistent effort so long after being taken from the water that it seemed impossible that the spark of life could still exist. Follow the above directions explicitly and, if there is still life, you will surely succeed in restoring the victim. Just keep at it.

As soon as the patient can swallow, give hot tea, coffee or milk. Spirits given too freely at this time might cause depression.

## DROPSY

A condition that may develop as a complication of various diseases, in which there is an accumulation of watery fluid in the cavities of the body or in the fatty tissues. This is caused by the filtering of the watery portion of the blood through the vessels, due to a slowing of the circulation or a damming up of the current. Inasmuch as dropsy develops following the disease of some of the organs, as the heart, liver or the kidneys, its treatment includes a stimulation of those organs as well as an attempt to carry off the fluid already accumulated.

The remedies prescribed for dropsy are various purgatives, digitalis, cream of tartar and Irish broom.

## DRUG HABITS

Medical science has been seeking for many years to discover a treatment that would remove the craving for opium, morphine, cocaine and alcohol. Many so-called cures for the habit of taking these narcotics have been and are still widely advertised. The victims of these habits are rarely ever cured by such treatments, and almost invariably are made worse off by taking them. The preparations given in such treatments are usually loaded with the very narcotics that they are supposed to fortify against.

There have been introduced into some of the leading hospitals and the practice of some physicians, treatments that are said to accomplish the desired object. They are said to obliterate the craving for the narcotic to which the patient has been enslaved. Such treatments consist in administering powerful drugs that quickly turn the system from its dependence upon the narcotic used, and then the treatment seeks to eliminate from the system the poison left by the drug or intoxicant habitually used.

Within a week or two the cure is supposed to be accomplished, and the patient, then weak from the effects of the treatment, has to be built up with nourishing food, proper exercise, bathing, fresh air and sunshine. Several months at least are required to firmly establish new habits, and the patient should be under observation and advice during that time.

The treatment used especially among the victims of the opium and morphine habit has proved effective for the cocaine habit, the alcohol habit and the cigarette habit.

## Cure Depends Upon Will

A permanent cure depends upon the man himself. A weak-minded, weak-willed, sickly, ill-nourished person is much more likely to take up the habit again than the strong one. The treatment simply gives the patient a chance for a new start.

The great trouble in dealing with narcotic habits has been not so much the treatment of the physical effects of the narcotic poisoning as the craving for more of the narcotic. This craving differs with the different narcotics.

The craving for morphine is described as a pain and hunger which must be satisfied; that for cocaine causes a nervous restlessness which may lead into insane passion, which cocaine alone can quiet. Craving for alcohol, beginning with a mental desire, continues steadily until one can think of nothing else.

## Causes of Drug Habits

The special causes for indulgence in narcotics vary. In cases of morphine, pain is the usual cause and the welcome relief from pain repeatedly secured leads to the formation of the habit because of the sure, soothing effects of the drug. Insomnia from any cause often leads to the taking of laudanum or other forms of opium, including morphine.

The cocaine habit is even worse than the opium habit. Its use comes through some quack medicine, perhaps a catarrh nostrum. It may follow or accompany the morphine habit for its stimulating effects. The cocaine victim becomes a nervous wreck in about five months at the longest.

The alcohol habit, although in many ways less serious than the drug habits mentioned, often causes greater harm to the body than the drugs, by reason of the selective nature of the poison. Some single organ may be affected and bear the brunt of the poison, while the others seem to escape. This may result in disease in the heart, liver, kidneys or brain, which may prove fatal.

The one word of advice to follow with reference to narcotics is to let them alone, except when prescribed by a physician for the relief of acute conditions, and then to beware of continuing taking such prescriptions longer than is actually necessary.

## DYSENTERY

Dysentery is an infectious inflammation of the large intestine, which appears principally in hot countries, but also prevails to a certain extent in temperate climates during the summer and autumn. Dysentery is caused by a number of different germs, the symptoms varying in intensity and character according to the infection, and augmented by changes in temperature, eating food that is partially decayed or other intestinal irritants. There is pain and tenderness in the bowels, frequent passages of mucus and blood, attended by tenesmus, fever and prostration.

The treatment should be rest in bed, fluid diet, small doses of castor oil at frequent intervals and applications of hot poultices upon the abdomen. In chronic dysentery a solution of one dram silver nitrate and one ounce distilled water, one teaspoonful of which, added to three pints of water, may be used as an injection. The disease, either acute or chronic, is dangerous, and should have the attention of a physician.

## DYSPEPSIA

This term is applied to symptoms of derangement of the stomach's functions. The symptoms are heartburn, gas, pain in the stomach, occasional rising of acid liquids from the stomach, feeling of heaviness in the region of the stomach, loss of appetite, irregular action of the bowels, and palpitation of the heart. There are a variety of causes. Among them overwork, either mental or physical, worry, hasty eating without proper mastication, overeating or indulgence in any food difficult to digest, or the symptoms may be due to some disease such as cancer or ulcers of the stomach.

The treatment should be directed toward removing the cause of dyspepsia, the diet should be limited to the most simple and easily digested foods, unless it is a nervous dyspepsia, when, oftentimes, the patient is not eating enough. Plenty of water should be taken to flush out the digestive tract. It is well to take some mild laxative and tonics, and then give nature a chance to work its own cure by rest.

## ECZEMA

An inflammation of the skin that occurs in both acute and chronic forms. The skin is reddened, thickened, itches and is covered with cracks or pimples or pustules. In some forms of the disease the skin is dry and scaly and in others moist. If neglected, the disease tends to become chronic. Eczema most frequently appears on the scalp and face, but it may appear upon any part of the body.

The diseased skin should receive antiseptic treatment. General treatment for the system varies in different cases, and should be under the direction of a physician. Often careful attention to the diet and other habits results in a cure. Tonics and laxatives are prescribed, inasmuch as the disease is caused by digestive or nervous disorders.

## EMBOLISM

A disease in which the flow of blood in a vessel is checked by some obstruction. It may be due to a clot of blood or a tissue thrown off which has entered the blood vessel, as a result of a tumor, inflammation or injury. When a blood vessel is thus obstructed it may cause inflammation or gangrene. or, if the blood vessel is a large artery, sudden death may occur. Obstructions of an artery in the brain are one of the causes of apoplexy. A little air entering the circulation causes embolism and sudden death may thus follow a surgical operation.

The patient should be kept quiet. Otherwise, there is little that can be done in the way of treatment for embolism. If the obstruction is in a vein the blood may find its way through other veins. In the case of a large artery, an amputation may be necessary to save life; but this may be unsuccessful.

## EPILEPSY

A chronic disease of the brain, manifesting itself in periodical attacks in which there is loss of consciousness and, usually, convulsions. Epilepsy, strictly speaking, is not a disease in itself, but the symptom of diseased conditions. Epilepsy may be due to injury to the brain, to the excessive use of alcoholic beverages, or to a severe fright, but is usually hereditary. The disease may appear at any time of life, most frequently during childhood. In a majority of the hereditary cases the cause traces back to alcoholism.

During a severe attack of epilepsy the patient cries out and falls unconscious. The head is bent back, the eyes are rolled upward and the face is distorted, becoming blue, owing to the difficulty in breathing, and the body becomes rigid; then violent jerkings of the muscles occur. There is frothing of the mouth, followed by a gradual relaxation and slowly returning consciousness. The attack lasts only a few minutes. One attack is not dangerous. Recurrent attacks are likely to lead to mental weakness and insanity.

## Little Can Be Done

During an attack of epilepsy all that can be done is to loosen the clothing, place a pillow under the patient's head and try to keep him from injuring himself. It does no good to sprinkle the patient with cold water, as in cases of fainting.

The only drugs that have an established value are the bromides. The treatment should always be under the direction of a physician. Of all things, never submit to treatment by a quack doctor or use so-called remedies that are advertised. The use of alcohol in any form must be avoided. A permanent cure requires the general building up of the system, establishing a good degree of nutrition, and improving nervous conditions. Cold baths are helpful.

## ERYSIPELAS

A skin disease accompanied by inflammation and fever. It is caused by germs which enter the body through some injured part of the skin or membranes. It may be either a large wound or through one so small as not to have been noticed, like a scratch or prick from a needle. Erysipelas appears most often upon the face, and usually starts from some injury of the mucous membrane of the nose. The first symptoms are usually a chill and general ill-feeling, followed in a day or two by high fever and the appearance on the skin, usually about the nose, of a bright, red, shiny swelling, which is hot and painful.

It spreads more or less rapidly, always preserving its sharply defined area. As it advances the swelling increases, frequently completely closing the eyes and frightfully distorting the face. There is much pain and intense burning. Vesicles and pustules usually appear on the inflamed surface and occasionally abscesses develop beneath it. In severe cases delirium often occurs.

The duration is from one to three weeks, the inflammation spreading and subsiding much like forest fires, leaving in its wake a mass of dead scales which are thrown off during convalescence.

## Antiseptic Treatment

In the treatment of this disease the greatest care should be taken against spreading infection. The patient should not touch the inflamed area, as by scratching he might easily convey the disease to other portions of the body. The affected parts should be kept covered by cool, soothing antiseptic dressings which are destroyed as soon as removed. In some forms of the disease it may spread over the greater part of the body.

Antiseptic dressings prescribed include the following: A solution of carbolic acid, one part to 100 parts water; a solution containing sugar of lead, two teaspoonfuls laudanum, and water one pint; or a saturated solution of boracic acid. Cloths wet with the solution used may be laid upon the inflamed surface and more of the solution poured on from time to time. If carbolic acid is used, it should be in the form of a weak solution, otherwise, there is danger of poisoning when applied to large surfaces of the skin. If symptoms of poisoning appear, the application should be at once removed.

Rest in bed, cleanliness and a light, nourishing

diet are essential until the skin has returned to its normal condition. As soon as erysipelas disappears the patient should take a series of hot soap and water baths and have a complete change of clothing and bedding. He should be moved to another room, if possible, also, while the room he has occupied is cleansed and disinfected.

## EYE DISEASES

The eye is a hollow globe covered with several membranous layers and filled with a transparent jellylike substance. It is situated in a bony case, and its movements are controlled by a number of pulleylike muscles. The eye may be likened to a camera. The cornea is a clear oval window in front admitting the light rays and refracting them toward a focus. The iris is a colored curtain stretched across the space just back of the cornea and contains an opening known as the pupil.

The iris, by dilating and contracting, enlarges and diminishes the size of the pupil according to the amount of light present and the distance from the object observed. The lens is a rather soft transparent structure situated back of the iris, and completes the refraction of the light rays, throwing a reversed image of the object upon the sensitive retina at the back of the eye, just as the lens of the camera does upon the photographic plate. The picture is then carried to the brains by the optic nerve, five branches of which spread out over the retina.

The nearer and smaller the object the more obliquely the rays strike the cornea, and, therefore, the more they have to be refracted by the lens to bring the picture closely upon the retina. This is done by the action of the ciliary muscle, which encircles the eyeball opposite the lens. This muscle, by contracting, increases the convexity of the lens and so increases its refractive power.

## Farsightedness and Shortsightedness

In a farsighted person the eyeball is too short, so that the image naturally falls back of the retina and to see nearby objects it is necessary to keep the ciliary muscle in constant contraction. This constant spasm of the muscle produces headaches and other discomforts, and is remedied by placing a proper convex glass in front of the eye to add the necessary refraction.

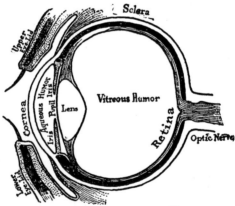

SECTIONAL VIEW OF THE EYE

In shortsighted persons the eyeball is too long, and a distant object falls in front of the retina so that a concave glass placed in front of the eye remedies the difficulty.

## Astigmatism

Astigmatism is a condition of the eye in which the surface of the cornea or lens is curved more in one direction than another, so that the rays of light are refracted unevenly and do not focus at the same distance, causing excessive strain upon the eyes and often blurred vision. This condition is remedied by a complex glass made to overcome the irregularity.

These three abnormalities of the eye and their combinations form the principal causes of eye strain, and one troubled with indistinct vision or subject to headaches or eyeaches after using the eyes should consult an oculist.

The eyes are very sensitive, and a little injury and a slight infection may lead to serious discomfort, impairment of sight or blindness.

## Conjunctivitis

Among the external disorders that affect the eye is inflammation of the conjunctiva mucous membrane that lines the eyelid. It may be a simple catarrhal inflammation or virulent suppurating inflammation, most common in new-born infants; or the serious granular process that is called trachoma.

The catarrhal inflammation, or simple conjunctivitis, usually arises from irritation of dust, chemical vapors, or eye strain. It frequently accompanies nasal catarrh or follows scarlet fever, measles and smallpox. There is increased flow of mucus and tears, reddening of the eyelids, and later pus may appear and the lids are stuck together mornings.

The treatment includes avoidance of aggravating causes, cleanliness and instillation of boracic acid solution.

## In the New-Born

Purulent conjunctivitis in the new-born is the result of infection from gonorrhea or some poisonous discharge of the mother, communicated at birth. If neglected the disease may develop in a few days so as to affect the cornea or transparent part of the eyeball and cause blindness. The treatment is cleanliness, cold compresses and the use of antiseptics under a doctor's direction. Great care should be taken if only one eye is affected to protect the other from infection. At birth a child's eyes should be carefully cleansed immediately, and a few drops of a 1 per cent solution of nitrate of silver in the eyes may prevent infection.

## Trachoma

Trachoma is a form of purulent conjunctivitis that produces an infectious discharge and is of a chronic nature. The membranes of the lid are red, thickened and undergo granular roughening. It is likely to result in a diseased condition of the eyeball and finally blindness. Trachoma is a very infectious and stubborn disease and should only receive thorough treatment at the hands of a physician.

## Inflammation of the Cornea

The cornea, which is a transparent outer coat at the front of the eyeball, may suffer from various forms of inflammation. Its nervous structure renders it very sensitive to light when inflamed. Serious inflammation of the cornea often follows injuries of the eye. A form of vesicular or pustular inflammation of the cornea appears frequently in children, due to improper nourishment and bad hygienic surroundings, and may follow certain diseases, as measles, scarlet fever, whooping cough and typhoid fever. Syphilis may cause a more serious internal inflammation of the cornea.

The general nutrition should be improved and the eyes should be protected from light by dark glasses. Pain may be relieved by hot applications. Treatment should be directed by a physician, preferably a specialist in eye diseases.

Ulcers of the cornea may follow injuries. Protection from light, hot applications and skillful antiseptic treatment are required. Abscess of the cornea is a form of inflammation attended by suppuration. Usually it follows some injury. The treatment should include good food, good air, hot applications, perhaps puncture of the abscess, and such remedies as a physician may find advisable. All such diseases threaten the sight, and may render necessary the removal of the eye.

## Scleritis

The sclera, the white coat surrounding the entire eyeball except the cornea area, is subject to inflammation, due often to uterine disorder in women, or rheumatic and gouty conditions in men, or perhaps to malaria or syphilitic taint. There is congestion appearing in the form of a dusky crescent on the outer side of the cornea, or purplish spots upon the whites of the eyes, dull pain and fatigue of the eyes. The cause should be removed if possible.

## Iritis

Iritis is an inflammation of the iris, the colored curtain lying between the cornea and the lens. It may be due to injury, syphilis, rheumatism or follow other infectious diseases. It comes on gradually with neuralgic pain through the eye, forehead and temples, and is worse at night. The eyeball is inflamed. The iris is cloudy and the pupil is small, irregular and sluggish. It is a serious disease and should not be mistaken for the milder and more superficial inflammations.

The patient should remain in bed with dry heat constantly applied to the head, and the pupils should be kept dilated with I per cent atropine. The medical treatment depends upon the cause.

## Glaucoma

Glaucoma is a disease which somewhat resembles iritis, but should never be mistaken for it, as the treatment is exactly opposite to that for iritis. It occurs in people past middle life. It usually has a period of several months preceding the attack, in which there is rapidly failing vision and a rainbow of colors is seen around a light. The onset usually appears suddenly, during the night, with severe pain in the eye and head, accompanied with fever, vomiting and prostration. Like iritis, the eye is inflamed and discolored and the pupil sluggish, but, unlike iritis, the pupil is dilated and the eyeball hard. This is a very rapid and dangerous disease and if not promptly treated leads to blindness.

The treatment of glaucoma, instead of dilating the pupil as in iritis, should be to contract it by dropping in the eye a solution of eserine, a grain to the ounce. This draws the iris away from the eyeball and permits drainage, relieving the tension.

## Cataract

Cataract is not, as many people suppose, a membrane which grows over the cornea, but is a cloudiness of the lens. It occurs most frequently in the elderly, due to long-continued eye strain, diseases which have impaired the general vitality or to the resulting changes of old age. Cataract appears slowly and the symptoms are those of gradually failing vision, sight being more distinct just at dusk for a time, the lens becoming harder and more opaque.

The treatment consists in waiting until the lens has sufficiently hardened and then removing it by operation. After healing has taken place, a strong convex glass is used to take the place of the lens removed.

The inner membrane of the eye or retina, the transparent vitreous body in the interior, the muscles controlling the eye, and the optic nerve, are all subject to diseased conditions too numerous to describe here. Such conditions may be indicated by impaired vision attended by pain, may lead to blindness, and require skillful medical treatment.

## Sympathetic Relations

It is well to remember that the sympathetic relation between the eyes may lead to the communication of disease from one eye to the other. Great care should be taken to prevent this. There is a sympathetic nervous relation between the eyes and other parts of the body, notably the brain, spinal cord, kidneys and stomach.

## Warnings

Eye strain, or other abuse of the eyes, is likely to lead to seriously impaired vision. Impaired vision results from a great many causes, and a remedy through medical treatment or properly fitted glasses should be sought early, by consulting an oculist. Delay is dangerous. Avoid quack eye doctors, spectacle peddlers and the use of eye washes not prescribed by a reputable oculist or physician.

## FAINTING

This is a loss of consciousness which comes on suddenly, caused by a decrease in the amount of blood supplied to the brain. It may be due to a great loss of blood from the body, violent pains, strong emotion, physical exertion or staying in an overheated or crowded room. The first symptoms are paleness, dizziness and ringing in the ears, objects appear to revolve around the patient. There is cold perspiration and sudden collapse, breathing and heart action become weak. This condition may last only a few seconds or several minutes.

The patient should be laid flat, with head low, and any tight garments loosened and a little cold water dashed upon the face. Plenty of fresh air should be allowed. Smelling salts or cologne applied to the nostrils help to revive the patient. As soon as one can swallow he may be given a little light stimulant.

## FELON

An abscess usually on or near the end of a finger. It is caused by bacteria which gain access through a slight injury. The abscesses form about the sheath of a tendon, or in the membrane surrounding the bone. A felon is always very painful, because of the rigidity of the tissues involved, and there is a considerable degree of heat and swelling. The treatment should consist of early and free lancing, and it is necessary to cut to the bone; in some cases, scraping of the bone is necessary— otherwise, the treatment is similar to that for boils.

## FLATFOOT

This is an inward rotation of the arch of the foot, so that the weight of the body rests too much upon the inner side of the foot. The principal cause is the wearing of ill-fitting and improper-shaped shoes. The treatment consists in restoration of the foot to its former condition by proper exercises. Sometimes special shoes or arch steel springs for the sole of the shoe are worn, but this should always be under the direction of a physician.

## FREEZING

The rule to follow in reviving a person who has been partly frozen is to induce warmth very slowly. The patient should be treated in a cold room. After removing the clothing, the frozen parts should be rubbed with snow or cold, wet cloths, or may be placed in cold water. The temperature of the bath or water applied should gradually be raised to 86 degrees in the course of two or three hours.

After the limbs have become more easily movable, artificial respiration should be resorted to if necessary. When the patient breathes naturally, he should be placed in an unheated bed and covered with blankets. The room should then be heated to a moderate degree of warmth. As soon as the patient is able to swallow he should be given stimulants.

## GASTRITIS

This is a catarrhal inflammation of the stomach usually caused by indiscretion in eating, or the excessive use of alcoholic beverages. There is loss of appetite, nausea, thirst, coated tongue, vomiting and pains in the stomach. The surface of the body over the stomach is sensitive to pressure and there is usually constipation.

The treatment should first be a clearing out of the digestive tract, after which the diet should consist only of fluids. It is often best to abstain, for a time, from both eating and drinking. Thirst and nausea may be remedied by swallowing small pieces of ice. Apply to the region of the stomach hot poultices, or a mustard plaster, which may remain until the skin becomes red.

In chronic cases of gastritis, it may be necessary to restrict the diet to milk chiefly for several weeks in order to guard against as well as cure. Any attack of the disease should be followed by a simple but nutritious diet.

## GERMAN MEASLES

An eruptive disease of childhood, sometimes mistaken for measles, but not related to it. Neither establishes immunity against the other. The disease is contagious and often epidemic. It is often of so mild a nature that the only symptoms noticeable are the eruption and a swelling of the glands of the neck under the ears. This swelling of the glands is one of the symptoms by which it may be distinguished from measles. The eruption also differs in that it appears first on the face, while that of measles appears upon the forehead before the skin of the face is affected. In German measles, also, the spots are paler red, average larger and are separate, while in measles they tend to run together in patches.

The eruption spreads rapidly over the body, and fades away, often all within 24 to 48 hours. In the more severe cases a slight cold in the head, cough, and sensitiveness of the eyes to light are symptoms of the disease that develop before the eruption appears. Unless fever develops, which is unusual, the disease requires very little attention, except to keep the patient separated from others to prevent spreading contagion.

## GOITRE

Simple goitre is an enlargement of the thyroid gland, which is located in the front of the throat just below the larynx. It is supposed to be due largely to some peculiarity of the drinking water. Aside from the unsightliness and inconvenience of the swelling, it may interfere with the breathing by pressure on the windpipe. If an excessive swelling occurs, removal of the thyroid gland by surgical operation is advisable. Medical treatment should be followed only under the direction of a physician. Some form of iodine is usually prescribed.

### Grave's Disease

Exophthalmic goitre or Grave's disease is an affection probably of nervous origin, characterized by a very rapid heart action, prominence of the eye-balls and enlargement of the thyroid gland. It may come on suddenly, following some violent emotion, as passion, fear or grief, but usually develops slowly, the first symptoms noticed being nervousness and palpitation of the heart. Protrusion of the eyeballs soon follows, often so great that the patient is unable to close the lids. The heart action becomes extremely rapid and irritable, and with these symptoms a goitre usually appears, gradually enlarging in size. As the disease progresses the patient loses flesh, becomes anæmic, and a severe turn of nervous symptoms develops.

The general treatment consists of rest and freedom from worry and excitement and the administration of certain heart and constitutional remedies. An operation for the removal of the gland should be performed when it produces pressure upon the laryngeal nerve, interfering with speech, or upon the large blood vessels of the neck, obstructing circulation, or, when the growth of the gland is very rapid and the heart and nervous symptoms severe.

## GOUT

Gout is a constitutional disease in which there is too much uric acid in the system. There is something wrong in the processes of transforming the nutritious elements of the food into body tissues, so that this poison, uric acid, collects in the blood and forms deposits about the joints, resulting in inflammation. This condition is sometimes hereditary, but is due largely to lack of exercise, overeating, particularly rich food, and excessive use of alcoholic drinks. Two forms of the disease occur—acute and chronic.

Acute gout begins with intense pains in the

joints, usually in the great toe, which is hot and swollen, and there is continued pain and fever. The patient is irritable and suffers frequent sudden pains and twitching of the muscles about the joints. Urine is scanty, high colored and contains a reddish deposit.

Chronic gout often follows the acute attacks with the other joints of the hands and feet involved. The chalky deposits slowly increase and deformities develop until the use of the members affected are very much impaired. Finally, death may result from inflammation of the vital organs, including either the stomach, liver or heart, perhaps.

## Diet and Habits

The treatment of gout involves, first of all, a thorough regulation of the diet and habits. The patient should have plenty of outdoor exercise and a light diet, consisting principally of fruits, vegetables, milk and butter. He should avoid beef, veal, mutton, pork and alcoholic drinks. Plenty of fresh water should be used both internally and externally.

During an attack of acute gout the patient should be put to bed, be limited to liquid diet, and alkaline drinks should be freely administered. The digestive organs should be kept regular. The limb affected by the gout should be kept raised, and bandaged so as to keep it warm.

Colchicum is the best remedy. This should be given under the direction of a physician.

## HAY FEVER

A catarrhal disease of the mucous membranes of the nose, throat and eyes. It manifests itself about once a year, at the same season, with the same person, usually in midsummer. It appears to be caused, in part, by the pollen of certain plants, the disease appearing only at the time when those plants are in blossom. It is supposed that the pollen enters the air passages and that certain oils characteristic of the pollen or parasites borne by it cause irritation of the mucous membranes. The symptoms are those of an acute cold in the head, with sneezing, watery discharge from the eyes and nose, itching and stuffed-up feeling in the nose and slight fever. Pains sometimes occur in the front and back of the head, while attacks of asthma are common. The trouble usually lasts several weeks and no permanent illness develops.

There is no sure cure for hay fever that has yet been found. It is sometimes relieved by spraying the nose with antiseptics or certain astringents. As a means of prevention, those who suffer from the disease find it desirable to go to localities free from hay fever when the time comes that they are likely to suffer from it. High altitudes in mountain regions are sought because there the plants whose pollen causes the trouble do not exist.

## HEADACHE

Headache is a symptom of many disorders. The proper treatment for permanent relief is treatment for the disorder that causes it. One of the most frequent causes is constipation, and in this case the right sort of diet is to be recommended rather than medicine. Another frequent cause is indigestion, and it is the stomach that needs attention. Eye-strain is a common cause, the pain usually coming along after steady use of the eyes. The only remedy is properly fitted glasses. In women, uterine troubles are often the cause of severe headaches. Headache may also be due to diseases of the nose or ear, various nervous conditions, exposure to the sun's rays, hunger and exhaustion.

Anyone subject to frequent or periodical headaches should have a careful examination made to locate the cause, and take proper treatment for its removal. Avoidance of stimulants, regulation of life, plenty of fresh air and exercise, are essential elements. For the relief of an attack of headache, rest in a darkened room, with cold applications to the head and hot water bag at the feet and the emptying of the digestive tract, are of service.

Use of so-called headache powders is a foolish practice. They contain poisonous drugs which may cause fatal diseases of the heart or nervous system. They may afford temporary relief, but they do not cure the disease which causes the headache.

## HEART DISEASES

The heart may be involved in a variety of diseases affecting the muscular walls or the valves, or the nerves that regulate the character of its beating. The muscular walls may be affected by overexertion, alcohol or poison from infectious diseases. Nervous trouble of the heart may be caused by indigestion, coffee or tobacco, worry or overwork. Diseases of the valves of the heart may be due to some defect in their formation at birth or to poison in the blood from various diseases, notably rheumatism. The valves may, by thickening or shrinking, fail to close properly, or the opening may stretch or become closed, which seriously affects the circulation, and, secondarily, the walls of the heart.

Heart diseases may be prevented by careful observances of the general rules of health. Overexertion should be avoided, especially when one is in a weakened condition. One suffering from heart disease should avoid excessive physical exertion, mental worry and the excessive use of stimulants. Plenty of sleep, rest and moderate exercise, fresh air, with deep breathing, help to improve the circulation in this instance, restoring the heart to a normal condition. Extremes of heat and cold should be avoided and it is important that the digestive organs are kept healthy and regular.

## Angina Pectoris

Angina pectoris is a serious heart disease, caused usually by a hardening and narrowing of the arteries that supply the walls of the heart with blood. It occurs in those past middle life. The attack begins suddenly, occasioned usually by some excitement or exertion. There is severe pain and sense of constriction in the region of the heart. The victim grasps at something for support, the face is pale and drawn with anguish, the whole body is covered with cold perspiration and respirations are absent or impaired. The pain extends from the heart region to the left shoulder, back, neck and down the arms to the fingers. The paroxysms last from a few seconds to several minutes, and are often followed by vomiting.

The treatment for the attack should be for the purpose of dilating the arteries. Inhaling the fumes of nitrate of amyl has a quick, relaxing effect upon the blood vessels. Anyone who has had an attack of angina pectoris should avoid exertion and always carry with him a little glass of capsules each containing five drops of amyl nitrate, and the instant the pain begins he should crush one of these in his handkerchief and inhale the fumes. Sometimes inhaling ether or chloroform, or a hypodermic injection of morphine, gives relief.

Angina pectoris, especially, and any other kind of heart disease, for that matter, should be treated by a physician without delay.

## HEAT PROSTRATION

This is due to a long exposure to high temperature. It occurs most frequently in those who are not in good physical condition. It usually comes on gradually with headache, faintness, nausea, cold perspiration and great exhaustion. There is a sighing respiration and rapid, feeble pulse. Sometimes there is a moderate elevation of temperature, but usually the surface is cold and pallid and the temperature is subnormal and frequently unconsciousness ensues.

Treatment in a mild form is rest and a gradual cooling of the body and mild stimulation. In the more severe forms where there is a great coldness of the surface the patient should be placed in a hot bath, rubbed briskly and stimulated freely. Perfect rest should follow an attack for a considerable period of time.

### Sunstroke

Heat or sunstroke occur from the same cause, but chiefly from exposure to intense heat of the sun while undergoing severe physical exertion. This is a much more serious condition, and is accompanied by a very high temperature. It may come on suddenly, the victim dropping unconscious, or may begin with severe pain in the head, dizziness, nausea, vomiting and sensation of great heat and distress, unconsciousness developing slowly. The face is flushed, the eyes bloodshot and the skin intensely hot; convulsions and delirium may ensue.

Every effort should be made to reduce the temperature. This may be done by means of a cold pack and cold bath, with an ice bag to the head, and a hot stimulant should be administered. Aromatic spirits of ammonia are sometimes used for this purpose. Care should be taken not to continue the applications after the temperature is sufficiently reduced. One attack always predisposes to another, so that care should be taken to avoid unnecessary exposure.

## HERNIA

Hernia is a descent of a portion of the abdominal contents, usually a loop of the intestine, through some natural or artificial opening in the abdominal wall. Hernia may be present at birth or come on later in life, occurring usually in connection with some sudden strain which forces the abdominal organ involved through the opening. The most common location of hernia is in the groin, where it pushes its way through the natural canal for the spermatic cord, or alongside of the large blood vessels as they descend through the abdomen into the leg.

The greatest danger from hernia is the possibility that the bowels may become caught in the opening and cannot be returned. If it is not soon replaced by manipulation or operation, death results in a few days. Well-fitting trusses may be worn to retain the hernia within the abdomen, but the only safe and sure treatment is an operation.

## HICCOUGH

This is a spasmodic contraction of the diaphragm —a large muscle which separates the chest from that of the abdomen—and by movements of which the air is drawn in and forced out of the lungs. The usual cause of hiccough is indigestion. It may also be caused by hysteria, fever or diseases of the brain. It is usually a slight disorder, and may be remedied by holding the breath until the spasmodic action of the diaphragm ceases. A glass of hot water or a little bicarbonate of soda often gives relief. A bandage tightly bound around the abdomen often stops hiccough in small children. If the trouble is too serious a physician should be summoned.

## HIVES

Hives is an affection characterized by the sudden appearance of a number of whitish, pinkish or reddish elevations upon the skin. These elevations resemble bee stings or insect bites and are attended with much itching and stinging. The trouble usually lasts only a few days. The cause is usually some intestinal poisoning, in many cases due to eating food difficult to digest. Strawberries and shell-fish sometimes cause it.

If the cause is known, as in the case of certain foods, they should be avoided. Relief can be obtained by bathing with a solution of baking soda or boracic acid. Vinegar or spirits of peppermint may afford relief. If due to digestive disturbance, a mixture of rhubarb and soda, or a dose of salts may be taken.

## HOARSENESS

Hoarseness is caused by catarrhal inflammation of the larynx. It may be relieved by dissolving hoarhound candy in the mouth; or the white of an egg, well beaten, to which has been added the juice of one lemon and sugar, is recommended, a teaspoonful being taken at a time.

## HOOK WORM DISEASE

This disease is confined to warm climates. It is due to the presence in the intestines of a thread-like worm which sucks the blood from the mucous lining and at the same time injects a virus which prevents the coagulation of the blood. When existing in large numbers in an individual they produce a chronic inflammation of the intestines, causing diarrhea, hemorrhage and profound anæmia.

The eggs of this worm pass out in the excreta and where the hygienic surroundings are bad, as among the poor of the southern states, they soon hatch out in the soil into minute embryo, which easily pass through the bare skin of the hands and feet of those coming in contact with them. Passing into the circulation, they are carried through the heart to the lungs; thence up the trachea and down the œsophagus to the stomach, and finally into the intestines, where they develop into mature worms.

The symptoms depend largely upon the number of worms inhabiting the individual and are much less marked in negroes than whites. There is weakness, anæmia, emaciation, apathy and craving for dirt and other indigestible substances. Prevention is wholly sanitary, consisting of a proper disposal of the excreta.

The treatment is thymol, the dose taken in the morning on an empty stomach. This stupefies the worms and a dose of epsom salts taken two hours later clears them out.

## A Plague of the South

This disease has recently been made a subject of special study by the government and medical research societies, but not until recent years has it been known that the disease was very prevalent in the southern states. The hook worm disease was formerly regarded as restricted to miners. It has been learned that a very large percentage of the so-called poor whites of the South and most of the lower class of negroes in that part of the country have the disease.

Often whole families are infected, where they live in unhealthful suroundings. Negroes are said to be much more susceptible to the disease than whites, but usually suffer less from it, so that the symptoms are less marked in negroes than in whites, as stated above. It is believed that much of the shiftlessness and lack of ambition among the poorer people of the South may be attributed to this disease.

## HYDROPHOBIA

This disease, known as rabies, is infectious and is communicated through the saliva or blood of animals suffering from the disease. It is usually., communicated by dogs. The first positive symptom of the disease may appear at any time between six days and eleven months after infection. There is first a feeling of choking in the throat and difficulty in swallowing. As the disease progresses, swallowing becomes more difficult and finally impossible, with painful spasms in the back of the throat and a sensation of great suffering there at the very sight of liquids. Breathing is painful, and there is feeling of suffocation. There is a constant flow of saliva and sticky mucus from the mouth and throat. There are usually convulsions, although the mental faculties are unusually clear until the last. Death usually results from exhaustion after a period of about four days. Recovery is unknown after the disease has once developed.

The first treatment following a bite of an animal suffering from hydrophobia should consist in tightly binding the limb above the wound, cutting out the tissues surrounding the bite, or at least cauterizing the wound with hot iron or caustics, such as caustic potash, nitric acid, or sulphuric acid. Unless the wound is thus treated within five minutes it is not likely to prove very effective.

## The Pasteur Treatment

The only cure is the early use of the Pasteur treatment. This method consists of treating the body with a preparation made from the spinal cords of animals that have been artificially inoculated with the disease. Many so-called Pasteur institutes are not reliable, but one at New York and one at Chicago have for some years been doing effective work.

## HYSTERIA

This is a violent emotional condition or brainstorm most common in women. The symptoms are nervousness, excessive crying and laughing, pains more or less general, lack of sensibility or choking sensations in the throat. There is often great mental excitement; sometimes delirium and convulsive attacks, in which there may be a stiffening of the limbs and loss of voice, sight and vision during the attack.

Many of the symptoms are due to the condition of the mind, and any strong appeal to the mind often brings relief. The treatment should be in the hands of a competent physician. Too much sympathy, anxiety or fussing over the patient should be avoided.

## INFANTILE SPINAL PARALYSIS

Anterior poliomyelitis, as the doctors call it, is an acute contagious disease, usually epidemic. It attacks children, oftenest between one and five years old, but may occur at any age. It appears from a few days to a month after exposure, and it is believed may be carried by an intermediate person. The disease is due to a minute germ, which enters the system, probably through the nasal passages, and causes an inflammation of the gray matter of the anterior portion of the spinal cord. This portion of the cord controls the muscular system, and the amount of paralysis following varies in proportion to the extent and severity of the inflammation.

The onset is always sudden, usually with fever, some digestive disturbance, pain and tenderness in the back and limbs and profuse sweating, followed in a few hours or days by paralysis of the muscles of one or more of the extremities. In most of the fatal cases the muscles of respiration are affected and the patient dies from inability to breathe. The paralysis reaches its height in a few days, and remains so for several weeks, when improvement slowly begins and lasts for six months or more.

Finally, there is often an arrest of growth in the affected limbs and the muscles become shrunken. Coldness, blueness and deformity of the limbs may result. The patient should be put to bed, and should remain absolutely quiet. The affected limbs should be kept warm and supported with cotton, splints and bandages. In a few weeks after the soreness has subsided they should be gently moved, massaged and the use of electricity carefully begun. The limbs should be held in correct position to prevent stretching of the muscles and deformity.

## INFLUENZA

It is a contagious disease commonly called the grippe, and appears in epidemic form. The symptoms of its approach are headache, a general sense of ill-feeling, followed by pains in the limbs, chills, fever, prostration and catarrhal symptoms of the respiratory tract. The disease may confine itself to these discomforts and pass away in a few days, or there may be a general prostration and inflammation of the digestive organs and nervous system, with excitement and sleepiness or unnatural drowsiness. Sometimes weakness of the heart occurs. There is danger of complications with pneumonia or pleurisy, and tuberculosis. Other organic diseases are liable to follow.

The patient should remain in bed until all symptoms have disappeared. The diet should be limited to milk or other foods that are easily digested. Early treatment should consist of brisk cathartics, hot applications and hot drinks to cause perspiration. During convalescence great care should be taken to avoid contracting cold, for a relapse may prove serious, because of the complications which may arise.

## INSANITY

Many diseases of the brain, due to many causes, result in unnatural conditions of mind that are called insanity. The disease may manifest itself in what is known as melancholia, which is a state of melancholy carried to an extreme degree, and often leads to attempted suicide. Then there is monomania, in which the victim is insane on some one subject. This may lead to serious consequences, although on other subjects the victim may be perfectly sane.

What is known as mania is a diseased condition of the brain in which the victim is subject to all sorts of illusions and hallucinations and the mind seems to be in a state of chaos.

Still another form of insanity is known as dementia. This sometimes develops among old people. It is a weakened condition of intellect and will power that may lead to complete imbecility. The insane may be quiet and harmless, or exceedingly excitable and violent to the extent of great danger to themselves and those with whom they come in contact.

The causes of insanity include abnormal conditions that may be inherited or any of the following:

Fevers, epilepsy, syphilis, masturbation, blows upon the head, worry, misfortune; religious, political or any acute or prolonged excitement; overstudy and lack of sleep.

## Treatment

The insane should be so treated as to have quiet and relief from whatever causes or aggravates the trouble, if possible. They should be carefully watched to prevent any violence.

No insane person is safe, and it is always best that they should be treated in a sanitarium or insane hospital, where conditions are suitable for the treatment of such people. To prevent insanity, it goes without saying that the things which are likely to cause it should be avoided.

## INSOMNIA

Inability to sleep may be due to many causes, including a condition of nervous exhaustion and approaching insanity. One of the frequent causes is the nervous conditions brought on by brain work or worry. Sleep may often be induced by physical exercise taken to the extent of inducing fatigue, but great care should be taken, of course, to avoid overexertion. Some vigorous work out of doors is recommended; sometimes a walk is sufficient; sometimes gymnastic exercises.

A warm foot bath just before retiring is often effective. Drinking a glass of hot milk just before retiring or when awakening at night is one of the best remedies for insomnia. This draws the excess of blood from the brain to the stomach.

A hot, wet pack is an effective remedy in desperate cases. This is applied by taking a large blanket and wringing it out well from hot water, wrapping it smoothly and closely around the whole body with the exception of the head, and around that adding dry blankets. The patient may remain in this an hour or longer if awake, or all night if sleeping.

The condition of the mind is important and the worries of the day should not be taken to the bed chamber. Drugs should be taken only as the last resort. The sleeping room should be dark and well ventilated. Quiet surroundings should also be secured if possible. If the surroundings are unnecessarily noisy, plugs of cotton should be placed in the ears during the night. Late hours should be avoided, and one addicted to insomnia should not only go to bed early but rise early.

## ITCH

It is due to the activity of a little pearly white insect barely visible to the naked eye, which enters the victim's body, usually when the latter is sleeping with someone afflicted with the disease. The female insect selects some soft protected part and begins burrowing head first into the outer layer of the skin until she has completely buried herself. She then deposits an egg and burrows onward just beneath the surface, laying one or more eggs per day for about two months, when she dies. Meanwhile the earliest-laid eggs hatch out and the young escape upon the surface to continue the tunneling process of their mother.

The symptoms of the disease are an intense itching of the skin at night, the warmth of the bed stimulating the insects to activity. The appearance varies from a slight eruption between the fingers, or a few scabs and scratch marks upon the abdomen, to that of long-neglected cases where the whole body, except the face, is a mass of scabs and pustules.

The treatment is simple and effective. Each night before going to bed scrub the afflicted areas thoroughly with hot water and soap and a nail brush. Dry and rub in a sulphur and lard ointment. The cure will be complete in three days.

## JAUNDICE

A condition in which there is some obstruction to the flow of bile into the intestine. The bile, secreted in the liver, unable to escape in the normal way, is taken up by the blood and carried to all the tissues of the body. This condition is apparent from a yellow discoloration of the skin and the whites of the eyes. Catarrhal jaundice is due to an extension of a catarrhal inflammation of the upper part of the intestines and usually also of the stomach to the bile ducts and a closure of the passage by a swelling of the mucous membrane.

Sometimes the flow of bile is stopped by the lodgment of a gall stone. In such cases there is intense pain, which may be intermittent until the gall stone works its way through. The pain caused by this latter disorder is known as biliary colic. It is necessary to administer morphine hypodermically, or to give chloroform by inhalation, to relieve the intense pain. Surgery is the most satisfactory treatment for gall stones. Jaundice may also be caused by pressure of a tumor upon the bile passage.

Thus it may be seen that what is known as jaundice is really a symptom of a variety of disorders which should be understood before treatment is undertaken. Great care should be given to the diet, and the bowels should be kept open by gentle laxatives and hot enemas. In all cases fatty foods should be avoided. Mineral and alkaline waters should be drunk freely. Warm baths should be taken in which a little soda has been dissolved, to relieve the itching of the skin which attends jaundice.

## LEPROSY

It is a chronic infectious disease, which affects the whole system, and runs usually for many years. There are two types of the disease. One characterized by formation of nodes in the skin and mucous membrane which finally soften and break down into ulcers. The other form is a disease of the nerves. Primarily reddish spots appear on the skin, which later become white and are insensible to touch. The area of insensibility spreads over most of the body. A wasting of the muscles occurs and they gradually become paralyzed and gangrene may result, which leads to a loss of fingers and toes, and sometimes the entire hand or foot.

In treating the disease, it is important that the patient should be separated from those not so afflicted, and he should be given such treatment as will maintain as high a degree of nutrition as possible. Cleanliness and good hygiene should be maintained. The disease responds to no known medicinal treatment.

## LIGHTNING STROKE

If actually struck by lightning the victim is usually killed outright. If the injury sustained from a stroke of lightning is not fatal immediately, there is a fair chance of recovery. The victim is usually unconscious and the pulse and respiration are weak. The face is pale, and the skin cold. Usually there is partial paralysis and more or less nervous pains.

The first treatment should be to loosen the garments, sprinkle cold water in the face, with the head kept low, while the body is vigorously rubbed. Smelling salts should be applied to the nostrils. Plenty of air should be provided and artificial respiration should be performed. Further treatment should be under the direction of a physician.

To avoid being struck by lightning, one should not seek shelter under tall trees that stand alone nor cross an open field during a thunderstorm. Telephone and telegraph poles should be avoided, and in a house one should keep away from large metallic objects and should not use a telephone. If there is a draught through open windows, they should be closed.

## LIVER DISEASES

The liver is the largest gland of the body and has several important functions to perform through which it is exposed to the liability to disease. The liver not only produces bile to aid in the digestion of fats, but helps to eliminate from the blood waste matter in the form of urea, which it passes on to be transferred to the kidneys for excretion. There are many disorders to which the liver is subject, but many of the ailments attributed to the liver are, in fact, disorders of the stomach and intestines.

Perihepatitis is an inflammation of the fibrous coat of the liver called Glisson's capsule. It may be caused by pressure of corsets, tight clothing or injuries from blows or falling, or from extension of inflammation from the gall bladder, or a gastric ulcer. It may also result from diseases within the liver. The fibrous coat thickens, and thus may cause compression of the liver substance, and, by extension of inflammation, may produce cirrhosis of the liver. As the capsule thickens, pain and tenderness develop, especially upon pressure. The treatment should include rest in a comfortable position. In the early stages of an acute attack an ice bag may be applied, followed later by hot applications.

### Congestion

Active or arterial congestion of the liver may be caused by overeating or overindulgence in alcoholic liquors, coffee or spices, or by infectious fevers, notably typhoid and malaria, or disturbed menstruation. The symptoms include the sensations of pressure, of fullness, and there may be pain. In severe cases swelling of the liver may compress the bile ducts and cause slight jaundice. Treatment should include rest, and, if the congestion is due to some other disease, that disease should be treated. If due to errors of diet, they should be corrected. The patient should abstain from food that stimulates the liver, such as alcohol, spices, and should reduce the amount of fat, sugar and salt taken. Vegetables and fruit should be eaten freely. Mild laxatives should be administered. Passive or venous congestion of the liver may be due to weakened heart action, chronic bronchitis, adhesions or contraction of the lung tissue, or may be due to obstructions within the liver. The treatment should be relief of whatever disorder causes the congestion.

Hepatitis is an inflammation of the liver, often a sequel to some of the infectious diseases, especially malaria, typhoid, erysipelas, blood poisoning, pneumonia and dysentery. It is especially prevalent in hot countries. Alcohol often contributes to this cause. The hepatic cells suffer poisoning and undergo degenerating changes. The symptoms are usually vomiting, diarrhea and if in the region of the liver, there may be mild or high fever, and in some cases there are chills. The first attack usually ends favorably in from eight to fourteen days. There is an inclination to later attacks which are generally more severe and of longer duration, and may end in abscess or some form of degeneration of the liver, with fatal outcome.

## Abscess of the Liver

Infection by some pus-forming bacteria may lead to abscess of the liver. Infection may be by ulcerative processes from adjacent organs, the most common examples being those from ulcers of the gall, bladder, bile ducts and stomach, or the infection may reach the liver by means of the blood currents. Among the symptoms of abscess of the liver are fever at irregular intervals with chill and high temperature, followed by sweat and weakness. The intermittent fever resembles that of malaria.

If near the surface, there is likely to be sharp pain. If deep in the liver, where sensory nerves are absent, there may be but little pain. There is nausea, vomiting, foul taste and coated tongue. In the case of abscess, the liver becomes considerably enlarged. Later the abscess may become firmly surrounded by tissue, so that symptoms are less pronounced and disintegration of the liver and poisoning may develop rapidly, leading to death.

The treatment, as in the case of other liver disorders, should include care with reference to the diet, avoiding irritating articles, especially drinks containing alcohol. In the early stages cold applications may help to reduce congestion, and later if there is severe pain hot compresses will be beneficial. Care should be exercised in the use of cathartics, which may have an irritating effect. Medicinal treatment should be strictly under the direction of a physician.

## Cirrhosis

Cirrhosis of the liver, or chronic interstitial hepatitis, is a slow inflammation of the liver which results in an extensive growth of a fibrous tissue that compresses and destroys the cells secreting needed fluids and seriously obstructs the circulation of the blood in the organ. The disease appears in two forms—the atrophic, in which the liver is reduced often to less than half its normal size, and undergoes some form of degeneration; and hypertrophic, in which the liver increases in size. The atrophic cirrhosis is often caused by habitual indulgence in alcoholic liquors, sometimes results from syphilis, sometimes follows malaria. In the early stages the symptoms are only those indicating dyspepsia.

Later, possibly some years after the disease has begun, there is pain, either dull or sharp, and it is possible to detect a decrease in the size of the liver. The patient's health and nutrition generally are much impaired and he becomes weak and sallow of complexion. The hardening and shrinking of the liver causes obstruction to the circulation through it, and results in a large accumulation of fluid in the abdomen.

In hypertrophic cirrhosis, as in the other form of the disease, the first symptoms are of a dyspeptic nature, followed after some months by painful enlargements of the liver. There is loss of appetite, nausea, vomiting and usually fever. The skin becomes jaundiced. As the disease progresses there are hemorrhages. Toward the end the appetite may increase, but eating seems to do no good, and the patient dies from general exhaustion. A termination of the disease may not occur for several years. The treatment should include avoidance of irritating articles of diet, especially avoiding alcoholic drinks, coffee and spices, and limiting the amount of fats, starch and sugar. A milk diet is often of benefit. Constipation should be treated by some means other than irritating laxatives, including in the diet fruit and vegetables for this purpose.

## Fatty Degeneration

Fatty degeneration of the liver is a disease in which the natural cells break down and change into fat, sometimes as a part of general obesity, sometimes in cases of anæmia and tuberculosis, sometimes because of the excessive use of alcohol, or through some form of poisoning. The treatment should be directed principally to relieving the disease which causes the trouble.

Waxy degeneration of the liver is found in

patients who have had some long, serious disease. Tuberculosis is the most frequent cause. Next to that comes syphilis, sometimes rickets, and some of the infectious fevers. The liver cells change to a hard, waxy substance, and the organ, as a whole, usually increases gradually in size, although sometimes it shrinks. There are no definite symptoms. The treatment consists only in trying to relieve the original disease.

### Tumors

Tumors of the liver may be either harmless or malignant, the former being very rare. The malignant tumors are forms of cancer that may or may not give rise to definite symptoms other than enlargement. There is a gradual loss of flesh and strength; later, digestive disturbances such as nausea and vomiting. Then some pain as the the growth advances. Treatment can only afford temporary relief and should be directed to keeping up nutrition and relieving pain. If undertaken early enough there may be relief through operation. In the case of benign tumors, no treatment is advisable unless their size is such that relief is needed through drainage, which requires operation.

## LOCKJAW

Lockjaw, or tetanus, is a disease caused by infection of a wound by a bacillus inhabiting the soil. It is especially liable to follow a gunshot wound if contaminated with dust or earth, or any punctured wound from a rusty nail. It does not interfere with the healing of the wound, but it enters the system, producing poisons which involve and irritate the nervous system, causing spasmodic contraction of the muscles, particularly about the head, neck and back. The disease may develop at any time between 24 hours and several weeks after the injury. Sometimes it takes the acute form, which develops rapidly and is fatal, and sometimes the chronic form, which develops slowly and is less likely to prove fatal.

The first symptoms that usually appear are pains in the back of the neck, followed by inability to open the mouth, because of the contraction of the muscles that move the jaw. Sometimes there is a chill, and a rapid pulse with fever is always among the symptoms. The spasms extend from one group of muscles to another, including those of the legs and the muscles that control breathing, spreading rapidly in the acute cases. In chronic cases there is no fever, and the contractions are confined to the jaw and some of the muscles of the back. All the muscles affected become very hard and pain is caused by the convulsions. The patient remains conscious. The disease may run for four to six weeks and end in death from exhaustion, or in the gradual recovery of the patient.

### Prompt Treatment

Unless treatment is given immediately after the infection, the disease is usually fatal. All wounds should be treated with absolute cleanliness and antiseptics should be applied to destroy any germs which might cause disease. For lockjaw, the wound should be carefully disinfected, and any foreign matter should be removed. Keep the patient in an absolutely quiet, darkened room, protected from noise and drafts of air. Chloroform may be inhaled to relieve the spasms and morphine administered to secure sleep. The patient should be fed through a rubber tube, passed through the nose and down the throat if there is not sufficient space between the teeth. Lukewarm baths should be given. Success sometimes comes from injecting a serum prepared from the blood of an animal that has been artificially infected, a principle similar to that of smallpox vaccination.

## MALARIA

This is a disease caused by a certain parasite in the blood, and appears in different forms according to the particular kind of parasite with which the patient is infected. There is what is known as malarial fever, intermittent fever, recurrent fever, fever and ague, chills and fever, all referring to the same general disease. A few years ago it was discovered that malaria is transmitted only by means of a certain kind of mosquito, which obtains the germs by sucking the blood from those suffering with the disease; that the germs develop in the body of the mosquito and are injected into healthy individuals by the insect.

After the germs enter the human body there is a period of incubation, at the end of which the parasite develops to the size of a red blood corpuscle. It then sporulates or divides into 15 or 20 segments which rapidly attain maturity. This process is repeated, causing alternating periods of chills and fever. If there has been but one infection from the disease, the periods are less frequent than in the case of more than one the same day. In some forms of the disease the symptoms recur every second day, in others every fourth day. With the repeated development of the germs, apparently, there is put forth in the blood a poisonous substance, as well as the parasites themselves.

In the temperate zone, malaria appears most frequently in the autumn; in the torrid zone, where malaria is most frequently found, it occurs in spring as well as autumn.

The disease tends to destroy the red cells of the blood. It causes enlargement of the liver and spleen, and affects the functions of the kidneys. It also may cause dilation of the heart chambers.

## The Chills and Fever

The first symptom is the chill, with headache, nausea, vomiting, and this usually occurs in the morning, lasting from one to two hours. Then comes the period of fever with high temperature, face flushed, skin hot and dry, tongue coated, foul breath, and full pulse lasting from a half hour to four or even six hours. The third period of the attack is that of perspiration. Sweat starts in beads on the forehead and extends over the body. This covers a period of from eight to twelve hours. Malaria may be attended by diarrhea, vomiting, catarrhal jaundice and eruptions on the skin in often-recurring attacks. In case of children there may be convulsions.

In the form of remittent fever, which is found chiefly in hot climates, the attacks are more severe than other forms of the disease. The fever does not entirely disappear, and the patient suffers from a feeling of lassitude, loss of appetite and irritability. They may lead to paralysis of the heart where the patient is much weakened.

## Quinine a Specific

The standard remedy and specific for malaria is quinine. This drug kills the germs. Following malarial fever the patient should enjoy outdoor life, and have a hearty diet to restore the depleted blood.

Inasmuch as mosquitos, which carry the disease from one person to another, breed in stagnant waters, proximity to such places should be avoided in selecting a home. It is always best to build houses upon as high ground as possible and to keep away from marshy ground and stagnant water. It is important to keep the general health at as high a standard as possible. Mosquitos breed in stagnant water, and the drainage of swamps, and the use of petroleum or kerosene upon stagnant pools destroys them. Mosquitos should be kept out of houses by thorough screening.

Those exposed to the danger of malaria often take from six to ten grains of quinine each morning after breakfast as a preventive.

## MASTURBATION

An unnatural practice of exciting the sexual organs. The habit may be formed by young children, but most often by youths during the period of adolescence, when physical conditions of childhood are developing into those of young manhood and young womanhood. Once begun, there is danger that it may be continued. Its effects are to weaken the sexual organs, the nerves and the general physical and mental powers. The habit may lead to insanity.

It may be caused by some local irritation or inflammation, or may result from impure teaching. Its continuance is accompanied by a morbid condition of mind, in which impure thoughts and desires are encouraged, and fears that the victim is suffering from serious disease are often entertained. This unnatural state is encouraged by the false modesty that restrains parents from talking frankly with their children about sex matters and warning them of the dangers that attend self-abuse and impure sexual relations.

## Bad Influences and Ignorance

In many cases the only information children receive with reference to sexual matters comes from impure associates and from the lurid and exaggerated advertisements of swindlers who pretend to cure sexual diseases. Companions who fill the young mind with vile stories and thoughts, vile or suggestive literature, obscene pictures and immoral shows, all tend toward the formation of bad habits of mind and body. Ignorance of the truth, ignorance of the vital dependence of virile and attractive manhood and womanhood upon natural healthy sex conditions, ignorance of the penalty that must be paid, are at the bottom of most sexual vices.

## Teach the Truth Frankly

Children should be taught early the plain truth with reference to their bodies, so far as they need to know it in order to avoid bad habits. They should be told as soon as they can understand about the sacred responsibility and mystery of the origin of life. They should be warned against self-abuse and all impurity.

When these things are discussed in a frank, pure way, the morbid curiosity that is often the cause of youthful errors will not exist. If parents are frank with their children, the children are more likely to be frank and honest in all things. The active, inquiring minds of young people should be trained to seek satisfaction in the things that are pure. High ideals should be set before them.

## Hard to Break Bad Habit

If any bad habit is formed, it is hard to break. Knowledge of the truth and kindly moral encouragement often bring forth sufficient will power to discontinue self-abuse. If this fails, the case should be put in the hands of a good, pure-minded doctor. As soon as any evidence of masturbation appears a doctor should make a careful examination to see if there is any diseased condition, constriction or irritation of the sex organs that needs to be remedied. If parents feel unequal to the task, let the first sex talk be given by the family physician.

## MEASLES

This is a very contagious disease, most common among children, which manifests itself in an eruption beginning on the face and spreading over the body. One attack of measles protects against the second, but not against German measles. The eruption of measles starts in the mucous membrane of the nose and eyes, and thence extends into the throat, where it may be seen best on the soft palate. This causes coughing, which is especially severe when it extends into the trachea and bronchial tubes. The eruption appears first as irregular red spots, which have a tendency to group into patches.

Among the symptoms that develop are sneezing, coughing, bloodshot eyes, followed in a few days by the eruption referred to. Fever develops according to the severity of the attack. The skin itches and burns and the patient is restless and uncomfortable. As soon as the eruption has fully appeared the fever subsides. The disease is usually a mild one, but there is always danger of complications.

The patient should remain in bed in a shaded, well-ventilated room. The bowels should be kept open and plenty of fresh water allowed. Itching of the skin may be relieved by applying cold cream. If the eruption is slow in coming out drinking hot lemonade and a hot bath may expedite matters. If inflammation of the eyes develop a solution of boracic acid should be dropped into them every few hours. The diet may be of milk, gruel, broths or beef tea.

Precaution should be taken after an attack of measles against bronchitis, pneumonia, inflammation of the eyes, ears or larynx, which may occur if the patient takes cold.

## MENINGITIS

### Spotted Fever

Cerebro-spinal meningitis, or spotted fever, is an acute, infectious inflammation of the inner membranes covering the brain and spinal cord. It is due to the presence of a minute germ. It attacks children more often than adults. It sometimes occurs in epidemics, but is not considered a very contagious disease. The attack usually comes on quite suddenly, with vomiting, high fever and convulsions. There is pain in the back of the head and along the spine, while the muscles of the neck are stiff and the head is drawn backward.

Delirium soon develops and great sensitiveness to light and noise, and spasmodic contraction of the muscles. Sometimes there is seen upon the face, chest, or all over the body, small reddish or purplish spots, which give the disease the name of spotted fever. In a few days the patient usually sinks into a stupor, with pupils large and inactive, and death soon follows.

The general treatment consists of keeping the bowels freely open and placing an ice bag to the neck, and frequent sponging of the body. By far the most successful form of medical treatment is the anti-meningitis serum recently discovered by Dr. Flexner.

### Serum Treatment

Serum is the liquid part of the blood. If a quantity of blood is withdrawn from the circulation, the red blood corpuscles and other substances thicken into a clot and settle at the bottom, leaving on the surface a transparent, straw-colored liquid. This is blood serum. It has been found by experiment that blood taken from one species of animal which has been immuned frequently has the power of destroying the most deadly diseases in another.

The blood of most animals acts as a poison upon the human tissues, but that of the horse is practically harmless. So the horse is made immune to meningitis by first administering small doses of the meningitis germs that have been largely deprived of their vitality, and then gradually increasing the quantity and strength until the animal is rendered incapable of taking the disease. Serum from a horse thus inoculated is injected into the spinal cavity of the person suffering from cerebro-spinal meningitis and in many cases a cure is thus effected.

The result of using this serum is, as a rule, that those who recover after being treated with it get entirely well, while those who recover from the disease without such treatment are often left with some permanent derangement; sometimes with blindness or deafness, sometimes with curvature of the spine, sometimes permanently paralyzed in the limbs or mentally deficient, and the severe headaches which accompany the disease in acute stages may continue indefinitely.

A tubercular form of meningitis occurs quite frequently among children. It runs a slow course that is always fatal.

## Simple Meningitis

Acute simple meningitis is an inflammation of the inner membrane surrounding the brain, due to extension or transmission of some inflammatory process elsewhere in the body. This form of meningitis is also usually fatal. The treatment in general is similar to that for the contagious form, except the serum is useless here. Much relief is often obtained by withdrawing a portion of cerebro-spinal fluid to reduce the pressure on the brain.

## MUMPS

This is a disease of the parotid gland, which is a large salivary gland situated in front of and below the ear. The disease is contagious and occurs in epidemics, chiefly among children. The interval after exposure is from two to three weeks. The disease usually begins with chilliness, followed by moderate fever. Pain and swelling in the region of the parotid gland soon appear; the swelling rapidly increases, usually affecting both glands and involving the whole side of the face and neck.

There is difficulty in moving the jaw, swallowing and speaking. The test for the disease is tasting a pickle or other sour food, which causes pain, by the sudden stimulation of the gland.

The disease is not serious, as a rule, and passes away in about a week. Sometimes there are complications, which appear in a swelling and inflammation of the other glands of the body. This is usually due to taking cold.

The treatment is chiefly in the line of keeping the patient quiet and comfortable, and avoiding taking cold.

An inflammation and suppuration of the parotid gland sometimes comes on in connection with other diseases; commonly, typhoid fever, blood poisoning and smallpox. In such cases it is much more serious than the contagious form known as mumps.

## NASAL CATARRH

In its acute form it is known as cold in the head. It is an inflammation of the membranes of the nasal passages. In its chronic form the membranes and underlying tissues become gradually thickened until there is more or less obstruction to the passage of air. The natural secretion becomes thickened and offensive, while still later the disease areas shrink away, the glands lose their functions and the dust inhaled mingles with the sticky secretion and dries upon the membrane. The odor may become very disagreeable. Catarrh is usually caused by cold. Frequent acute attacks lead to chronic catarrh.

Acute catarrh is best treated by the ordinary remedies for cold, and the best treatment for chronic catarrh is frequent cleansing of the diseased membranes by alkaline antiseptic sprays. One suffering from chronic catarrh should have good air and plenty of outdoor exercise. So-called cures in the form of patent medicines are fraudulent and usually injurious. Many of these contain the dangerous drug cocaine and may lead to the cocaine habit.

## NERVOUS PROSTRATION

This term is used to indicate the condition of nervous exhaustion or weakness of the nervous system. There is a feeling of weakness, depression, irritability, inability to apply one's self to anything, difficulty in sleeping, usually headaches, backaches, and more or less neuralgic pains. In some cases there is a close approach to insanity, the nerve weakness extending to the brain. The disease may be often partly hereditary, and result from overwork and worry; from unhealthy habits of life, excessive use of stimulants and narcotics, or lack of sleep and overindulgence in social pleasures.

The existing cause should be removed. If the patient is completely exhausted, the best treatment at first is to place him in bed in a quiet room where only the nurse and physician shall see him. Absolute rest to body and mind, with plenty of nourishing, easily digested food, and massage and electricity to maintain the strength are necessary.

Later on, in milder cases, a quiet resort should be sought, and mild, healthy outdoor exercise should be taken, gradually increasing the exertion; and so-called nerve tonics, such as phosphorus, iron, strychnine and arsenic, may be administered.

## NEURALGIA

A painful condition of the nerves. The nerves most frequently affected are located in the face, and often the pain is felt around the eye and that part of the face just below the eye. Neuralgic pains of the chest somewhat resemble those of pleurisy. The sciatic nerve, running from the back part of the hip to the foot, is often subject to neuralgia. There may be swelling and soreness as well as pain in the part of the body affected.

Among the causes of neuralgia are anæmia, gout, rheumatism, diabetes, decayed teeth, various poisons in the blood, infections, exposure to cold, malaria, fatigue, mental shock and injuries. Children never suffer from neuralgia, and it is rare in extreme old age. Women suffer from it more frequently than men.

The principal symptom is pain, which usually appears in short attacks of great intensity. Although chiefly following the course of the nerves, neuralgic pain affects adjacent tissues. Heat as well as cold generally increases it; so does a light touch. Firm pressure sometimes causes relief. Numbness may accompany the pain, as well as muscular spasms in rare cases. The pain is usually increased at night.

The treatment should consist in removing any exciting cause, if possible, and improvement of the general health should be sought. Quiet and rest careful attention to diet, and keeping the bowels open are important. Sometimes relief is obtained by hot applications, menthol, camphor, mustard or painting upon the skin a small amount of cantharides in collodion. In severe, persistent cases a cure may be accomplished by an operation for the removal of a part of the affected nerve.

## OPIUM POISONING

The use of products of opium, especially morphine, either to relieve pain or as a habit, may result in acute or chronic poisoning. An overdose of morphine, or of opium in any of its forms, results in these symptoms of poisoning; sleepiness, contraction of the pupils of the eyes, slow, heavy breathing, perspiration and stupor. There may also be faintness. It is of the greatest importance to keep the victim awake. The treatment should include giving a strong emetic to induce vomiting, and strong coffee should be given as an antidote. Dash cold water in the face, and, if breathing stops, use artificial respiration. A physician should be summoned as soon as possible.

Chronic poisoning that results from the morphine habit is suffered by those who take the drug habitually. The habit may have its origin in taking morphine, laudanum, paregoric, or any sleeping preparation containing opium. Habitual use of these drugs causes a condition in which the system becomes dependent upon them. There is increasing nervousness, various pains, loss of appetite, and the mind eventually becomes affected. A hopeless wreck of the entire system can only be prevented by breaking off the habit.

This subject is further considered under Drug Habits.

## PELLAGRA

A blood disease unrecognized in this country until recently, although prevalent for many years in Europe, the exact nature of which is not yet fully understood. The disease appears first as a roughening of the skin, which later peels off, leaving the surface as it would after a scald. A sore mouth is one of the first symptoms of the disease and there is difficulty in swallowing. The patient becomes emaciated and weak, irritable and easily excited and then often insane. Pellagra usually progresses slowly and may continue for several years. Death may follow within a month or so after insanity develops. Abroad, about 10 per cent of those suffering from the disease become insane; and more than one-half die. The disease is sometimes taken for eczema, scurvy or leprosy. It is not considered contagious.

The disease appears among poor people in insanitary surroundings and in insane asylums and charitable institutions where cheap grades of food are supplied. There has been a theory widely entertained that pellagra was caused by eating moldy corn. Investigations by scientists, especially those employed by the government, have made it appear doubtful if this is true, although many cases have appeared where cheap grades of corn have been the chief article in diet. Poor quality of food, with not enough variety, may contribute to conditions that invite this disease as well as many others.

The most plausible theory as to the cause of pellagra is that it is carried by an insect as malaria and yellow fever are carried. Investigations indicate that abroad, where the disease has so long prevailed, the Italian midge bites a person suffering from pellagra and that the poison or germs of the disease in the blood is communicated by the insect to another person bitten later. In the United States the pellagra insects are thought to be the buffalo gnat, that is most prevalent in the lower Mississippi valley and the simulum black fly, that is found in many parts of the country.

The treatment most successful includes improving sanitary conditions, providing a diet of nutritious and easily digested food, and attempting to raise the tone and vigor of the system. No specific remedy has yet been put forward.

## PERITONITIS

This is an inflammation of the delicate membrane which lines the abdominal cavity and covers all the organs contained therein. It may be acute or chronic. Acute general peritonitis is often caused by extension of a local inflammation which develops in the appendix, Fallopian tubes or other organs, or may follow perforation of an ulcer in the stomach or intestines, or may be due to injury or obstruction of the bowels.

The symptoms include pain and tenderness in the region affected, distention of the abdomen, stiffness and vomiting. There is weakness, fever and a rapid pulse.

The treatment depends upon the cause, and is usually surgical. The disease is a very serious one, and should have the attention of a physician or surgeon immediately.

Chronic peritonitis may develop from an acute attack, but is often of tubercular origin.

The symptoms of tubercular peritonitis are pain in the abdomen, alternating diarrhea and constipation, or loss of flesh, occasional fever, and a gradual distention of the abdomen. Frequently there is little pain.

The treatment should be with a view of building the patient up in every way. There is a fair chance of recovery in such cases, but it may be necessary to perform an operation, removing the fluid and allowing the air to enter the cavity.

## PILES

Piles or hemorrhoids are little tumors, each consisting of a dilated vein which appears just within the margin of the anus. These tumors sometimes prolapse and appear externally and are known as external piles. There is frequently bleeding from internal piles. The external rarely bleed, but they are painful and cause a great deal of annoyance.

Piles may often be prevented or benefited by keeping the bowels regular. The diseased part should be kept carefully cleansed with antiseptics, and for external cases a tincture of equal parts of tannin and glycerin may be applied on a pad of gauze, wet with a solution containing two teaspoonfuls of sugar of lead, one teaspoonful of laudanum, and one pint of water.

The more severe cases require the removal of the hemorrhoids by operation. When properly performed the operation is not dangerous, and gives complete relief.

## PLEURISY

Pleurisy or pleuritis is an inflammation of the membrane or pleura, which covers the lungs and lines the inside of the chest. It is smooth and glossy and moves over the chest wall without friction. Inflammation causes roughening of the surface and the movements of these rough surfaces upon each other causes pain. Pleurisy may develop from inflammation of the neighboring organs or as a complication of other constitutional diseases; or it may be caused by a severe blow upon the chest, fracture of a rib or exposure to cold.

The symptoms of acute pleurisy are chill, fever, a dry cough and a sharp stitching pain in the chest with each respiration. The dry stage of pleurisy is often followed by a secretion of fluid which fills the pleural cavity, compresses the lung, displaces the heart and causes considerable difficulty in breathing. In severe cases the formation of the fluid may lead to rupture either into the lung or abdominal cavity.

The patient should remain quietly in bed and removal of the fluid must be accomplished under the direction of a physician. An operation sometimes becomes necessary.

## PNEUMONIA

This is a very prevalent and fatal disease, is an acute inflammation of the lungs, but particularly due to the invasion of a germ known as the pneumococcus. Its seriousness depends upon the extent and degree of inflammation, upon the age and general condition of the patient. Probably in the majority of cases it is not preceded by a cold, but a sudden chill enables the germs to successfully attack the lungs. They multiply very rapidly and form poisonous substances which affect the whole system. One or both lungs may be affected.

Pneumonia sometimes develops in the course of other diseases such as grippe, bronchitis, measles, whooping cough, smallpox, and typhoid fever.

The symptoms usually appear suddenly. There is a sharp chill followed by high fever and rapid pulse. A dry cough develops with a sharp pain on the side affected. Soon there is expectoration mixed with blood, giving it a rusty appearance. The breathing is short and very rapid. There is weakness of the heart and general prostration, and sometimes delirium. In about a week the crisis appears. The fever suddenly leaves and in favorable conditions recovery follows rapidly.

If the disease is prolonged there is likelihood of tuberculosis. In old people or children, or where the disease follows grippe, it runs longer than is usual in ordinary cases, but the symptoms are not so violent. Death may follow from heart failure, and as the crisis approaches it may be necessary to take rigorous steps in the way of stimulation. This should be done under the careful direction of a physician.

During the run of the fever the diet should be fluid preferably. For the most part milk. Water should be given freely. The room should be cool and well ventilated. Oxygen and heart stimulants should always be at hand. With the decline of the fever a more liberal diet can be given.

## PTOMAINE POISONING

This is a dangerous kind of intestinal poisoning which may result from eating any animal foods that have begun to decay. Meat, fish, oysters, clams, lobsters, cheese, milk and ice cream are among the foods that make trouble. One should always avoid eating any food, especially of animal origin, that shows evidence of decomposition.

The symptoms consist of severe cramps in the

abdomen, nausea, vomiting and violent diarrhea or in some cases constipation, thirst, headache, dizziness and chilliness, followed a little later by extreme prostration, difficulty in breathing and sometimes paralysis and convulsions. The disease may develop within half an hour after the spoiled food has been eaten or at any time within 24 hours.

As soon as there is suspicion of ptomaine poisoning a physician should be speedily called and emetics and cathartics should be given to empty the digestive canal. This should be followed by hot baths and remedies to stimulate the heart action. The effect of the poison is to weaken the heart, and the two purposes to be aimed at are the elimination of the poison from the system and to keep the heart

## RHEUMATISM

The disorders known as rheumatism manifest themselves in a variety of ways and are due to a variety of causes. There is acute articular rheumatism, which is also known as inflammatory rheumatism, or rheumatic fever. There is chronic articular rheumatism, both acute and chronic, Rheumatism is supposed to be caused by bacteria that develop through the failure of the system to throw off waste matter as it should.

In articular rheumatism, the bacteria apparently lodge around the joints and there is great pain, tenderness and swelling, with fever and sweat. The joints are usually affected, one after the other, often in rapid succession.

Chronic rheumatism develops from succeeding attacks of the acute disease, which lead to permanent changes in the tissues. There is thickening and roughening of the membranes, ligaments and ends of the bones, producing more or less stiffness and deformity of the joints, with painful and limited motion of the limbs. General nutrition is hindered and the victim becomes a chronic invalid.

Muscular rheumatism is a condition in which there is pain and difficulty in moving the muscles affected. It frequently affects the large muscles and small ligaments of the back, and then it is called lumbago. In addition to lumbago, it frequently affects the muscles of the neck, shoulders and chest. The greatest danger from rheumatism is that it may affect the heart.

The treatment for rheumatism should be under the direction of a physician. Complete rest in bed is necessary. The affected joints should be enveloped in cotton and bandaged and placed upon the pillow. Warm baths and hot air baths are beneficial. Water should be drunk in liberal quantities and the diet should be simple but nutritious. One of the drugs most frequently prescribed is salicylic acid. Strong drugs and patent medicines for rheumatism should be avoided.

## RICKETS

This is a condition in which the bones are soft, because they do not contain enough lime salts. This disease is usually in children during the first two years of life. The appearance of the teeth is delayed; the long bones of the body are noticeably soft and tend to curve. The form of the chest changes by increasing in diameter from the front to the back and narrowing from side to side. The forehead is often bulging; bow legs occur usually.

There is often restlessness at night, perspiration,

constipation, and an increase of urine. Sometimes there is diarrhea; and sometimes coughing. Convulsions are sometimes among the symptoms. Children having the disease are disinclined to sit up and the hair tends to fall out. Rickets are usually due to improper feeding and insanitary surroundings.

Plenty of nourishing food, and keeping the patient out-of-doors as much as possible, are the more important things to include in the treatment. Cod liver oil is often given. Great care should be given to the matter of cleanliness, sunlight and fresh air.

## RINGWORM

This is caused by a fungus growing upon the skin. It appears in round or oval, red or brownish, slightly elevated, scaly patches. The disease is contagious and may be communicated from one person to another by contact, or the diseased patches may multiply upon the same person. As the disease progresses the fine scales are noticeable and there is a tendency to heal in the center while the fungus spreads at the edges.

The treatment may be applications of tincture of iodine; sometimes two or three applications are sufficient. When the disease appears upon the scalp it penetrates the skin to the roots of the hairs, which, becoming brittle, break off or fall out. In such cases it is much more stubborn and more difficult to treat successfully and requires months or years to effect a cure.

The application of sulphur ointment is sometimes effective. If the disease does not yield promptly to home treatment a physician should be consulted, as it tends to become chronic, and the infection spreads.

## SCARLET FEVER

This is a very contagious disease among children. There is a fine scarlet rash, which appears upon the mucous membrane of the throat and spreads over the body and limbs. The cheeks have a peculiar bright red flush and there is apparently paleness along the nose and upper lip. The first appearance of the eruption is upon the soft palate and walls of the throat. The eyes are bright and there is not the swollen appearance which usually goes with measles. The tongue is coated at first, and then appears bright red with enlarged papillæ, known as the strawberry tongue. The symptoms also include headache, sore throat, chilliness, nausea and fever. Sometimes the first symptom is vomiting.

In mild cases, as the disease disappears, there may be very little scaling, but in severe cases there is considerable inflammation of the skin and the upper layer comes off in sheets. The kidneys are often affected in the later stages by the poisoning, causing acute inflammation of those organs.

The patient should have fluid diet during the fever period. He may be sponged with tepid water daily. Water should be drunk freely. Cold cream or cacao butter may be applied to the skin following the bath, after scaling begins. During the period of recovery it is important to still restrict the diet to simple food.

There is great danger of complications, including kidney trouble and inflammation of the middle ear. Sometimes there is loss of hearing. Chronic heart disease is also among the possible results of scarlet fever. The germs of the disease are difficult to exterminate and special care should be taken in the matter of disinfection. The patient should be strictly quarantined and all treatment should be under the direction of a physician.

## SCROFULA

A term formerly applied to a chronic enlargement of one or more lymphatic glands, now known to be due to tubercular infection. It occurs usually in childhood. It most frequently affects the glands of the neck. The child is usually weak, anæmic, perspires freely, and may suffer from tubercular conditions of the long bones. The lymphatic glands affected become hard, painless lumps. Sometimes they gradually disappear and sometimes they gradually soften and break through the skin with a puslike discharge. These openings sometimes remain as running sores for a long time. The membranes of the nose and ears are often affected, and deafness may result. If neglected, the disease is likely to lead to tuberculosis of the lungs or other vital organs.

The treatment should consist in building up the system and the diet should include the most nutritious foods, including eggs, milk and cream in liberal quantities. Cod liver oil is also given. The patient should have as much outdoor air as possible, and a cold sponge bath in the morning. The infected glands should be removed by operation before suppuration results.

## SEA-SICKNESS

It is due to a nervous condition caused by disturbance of the canals in the inner ear which are for the purpose of keeping a person in equilibrium.

It results from the motion of the ship upon the water. The symptoms include dizziness, pallor, violent nausea, chilly sensations, prostration, and vomiting.

It is well to remain on deck as much as possible and to seek fresh air. The condition of the mind is important, and if it can be directed away from the discomforting thoughts of seasickness and fear of the disorder, one is always better. In taking any medicine for seasickness one should remember that the trouble is not primarily in the stomach, and remedies for stomach trouble are useless.

## SEXUAL DISEASES

Two of the most serious diseases from which erring mankind suffers in this world are results of impure sexual relations. They are called gonorrhea and syphilis. These diseases, in very rare instances, may be contracted through toilet rooms, barber shops, soiled towels and public drinking cups. But infection, as a rule, is traced to intercourse with some person suffering from the disease in question.

The habitually or occasionally impure in sex relations are almost always more or less infected with disease. The practice of promiscuous intercourse leads surely and often immediately to this painful penalty. The germs of sexual diseases are so virile that exposure to them is almost sure to cause trouble and to remain in the system unless subjected to the most vigorous and thorough treatment. These diseases are exceedingly distressing and loathsome, and involve some of the most delicate, sensitive and vital organisms of the body. In advanced stages any organ may become involved. Insanity often results from this cause. No state of disease is more pitiable.

## Suffering of the Innocent

The scriptural declaration that the sins of the fathers shall be visited upon the children unto the third and fourth generations is literally true. Many innocent wives suffer because of the sins of their husbands, and their children and children's children suffer from the hereditary taint. This is the cause of many physical and mental wrecks, so born into the world. Babies frequently become blind from infection of the eyes at birth.

Safety from these diseases lies only in purity, and caution with reference to things by which infection might be carried to the innocent.

## Good Physician Needed

Upon the appearance of the first symptoms of any disease of the sexual organs a good physician should be consulted at once. His treatment should be followed until he pronounces the disease cured. No experiment should be made with home treatment. Delay and wrong treatment contribute to the seriousness of the case. Never consult a quack doctor who advertises to cure such diseases. Reliable doctors do not advertise. The ethics of the profession forbid the publication of anything more than a simple business card. The people who advertise are swindlers.

## SHINGLES

This disease is a nervous disorder attended by pain and eruption of the skin along the course of a nerve near the surface. The nerves along the ribs are most often affected. It is due to an inflammation of the nerve and the eruption appears with burning, itching, pain, and numbness along the course of the nerve affected. Sometimes shingles involves the eye, and may lead to blindness.

The treatment should include rest, warmth, and the use of soothing applications.

## SMALLPOX

An infectious disease characterized by a serious eruption. Although it somewhat resembles chicken pox in appearance it is much more severe and develops from papules which turn to vesicles and then to pustules, the same condition prevailing throughout wherever the eruption appears upon the body, and there never is a mixed condition. In chicken pox the eruptive condition is mixed, and because of this fact it is comparatively easy to distinguish between the two diseases. Smallpox manifests itself first by severe pain in the back and fever. Then the eruption first appears upon the forehead, spreading over the body. There is chill, fever and headache; sometimes stupor and delirium may follow.

The development of the disease is attended by the changes in the eruption. The small, hard papules that feel like bird shot under the skin finally become pustules, which tend to run together. In the later stages weakness of the heart sometimes causes death.

The treatment should include rest, coolness, pure air, softened light, and cooling beverages. The diet should consist of fluid foods. The mouth should frequently be washed out with a solution of boracic acid, and the skin should be sponged daily, using boracic acid solution about the eyes and face. Olive oil or vaseline may be used to relieve the itching as the eruption of the skin dries.

The patient should be quickly quarantined, and disinfectants should be used constantly in the sick room. Everything with which the patient has had to do should be destroyed finally.

Smallpox usually occurs among people who live in insanitary conditions and do not give proper attention to cleanliness. Cleanliness is an important precaution. Vaccination is usually a safeguard from the disease for a period of five years or more, although it does not give absolute immunity.

## SNAKE BITES

The principal poisonous snakes of this country are the rattlesnake, the American moccasin snake, and the copperhead. Most snakes are harmless. Snake bites are dangerous only when inflicted by poisonous snakes. The snake forcibly injects into the wound through the hollow or grooved fangs, its venom. If the wound is deep it enters immediately into the system through the blood, and so powerful is the poison that sudden physical and mental collapse may come at once. If the wound is slight the result of the poison comes more slowly and effects are not so immediate.

The usual symptoms are severe pain in the wound, swelling and discoloration of the skin around it, muscular weakness, and feeble, rapid pulse, coldness of the extremities, cold perspiration, headache, difficulty in breathing, nausea, and if the result is to be fatal, convulsions, unconsciousness and death. In fatal cases the swelling spreads extensively. Death may occur in an hour or may be delayed for several days.

## Vigorous Treatment

The treatment should be immediately binding the limb that has been wounded above the wound, tying as tight as possible. The wound may be sucked, if there are no abrasions on the lips or in the mouth. It is usually well to cut out around the wound about three-quarters of an inch. Then a red hot iron, live coal or a solution of permanganate of potassium may be applied. These destroy the tissues which contain the poison and the poison itself.

A solution of permanganate of potassium, one grain to an ounce of water, may be injected into the flesh around the bite for the purpose of destroying such poison as may be found. Lives are sometimes saved by immediate amputation of a bitten finger or toe. Stimulants should be given to encourage the heart action. In the case of children, care should be taken not to give an overdose of alcohol.

In India, where the cobra kills so many people, immunity has been secured by inoculation with the serum from animals bitten by the cobra. A solution of chloride of lime has been used with some success hypodermically for cobra bites in India. The success of treating snake bites depends largely upon immediate action.

## SORE THROAT

A simple sore throat may sometimes be cured by tying around the throat a handkerchief wrung out of cold water, over it being tied a woolen cloth, which should remain overnight. The throat should be gargled with a solution of salt and water or some good antiseptic, such as dioxygen or listerine.

## STINGS

The stings of bees or other insects cause painful sensations. The treatment should include the removal of the sting that has been left in the skin, and a solution of washing soda or ammonia water may be applied. Wet clay is often an effective remedy.

## STRAW ITCH

An eruptive disease of the skin, caused by the attacks of a small mite that infests straw and grain. The disease is new to American physicians. It has been reported in Indiana, Ohio, Pennsylvania, Maryland and New Jersey. The straw itch mite performs a useful service by preying upon certain insect parasites that infest straw and grain. When the mite becomes abundant and the opportunity presents itself, it attacks the laborers in the field, or the men engaged in threshing, or, perhaps, some city dweller who tries to sleep on a straw mattress, the contents of which carry the mites.

The straw itch mite is kin to the harvest mites known as the "red bug," which may also attack man, and to the common itch mite. It is of a yellowish-white color, of almost microscopic size. Unlike the common itch mite, it does not burrow in the skin, but attaches itself by means of claws and sucking disks with which the feet are provided, and while attempting to obtain nutriment it bores into the skin and injects some irritating poisonous substance, which results in local and sometimes constitutional symptoms of disease.

There is severe itching, and an eruption appears. A vesicle forms, surrounded by a circle of pink;

the vesicle is usually about the size of a pin head. It soon becomes a pustule. The eruption is most abundant on the body, and appears only slightly on the face and extremities. In severe cases there may be chilliness, nausea and vomiting, followed for a few days by a slight increase of temperature. In the milder cases, there may be only a lack of appetite, or there may be no constitutional reaction at all.

## Easy to Dislodge Mites

The mite is easily brushed off from the skin or crushed. As soon as removed, the symptoms rapidly disappear, and all signs of eruption will fade away in a week or ten days, even without treatment. Where the cause is not recognized, the patient will continue to suffer until the mites have all hatched out from eggs laid upon the surface, and all have died—a period of from three to seven weeks.

In treating the disease, contact with suspected straw or grain must be discontinued. The clothing should be completely changed. Inasmuch as the mite is easily brushed from the surface, it is hardly necessary to apply any preparation to kill it there. If desired, however, a mild sulphur ointment answers the purpose. For the eruptions, mild alkaline baths, soda and water, are good; or some soothing ointment, such as zinc oxide, is prescribed.

Mites remaining in the clothing that has been removed do not survive more than a day without food; airing the clothes for a day or two is sufficient to free them from danger. The mites are easily killed by heat or fumigation with sulphur or formalin.

## ST. VITUS' DANCE

This is a disease of the nerves which causes twitching of the muscles. It occurs chiefly among children. In many cases there are spasmodic contractions of the muscles of the body; sometimes limited to one side; sometimes on both. The organs of speech are affected so that talking is difficult. There may be weakness of the limbs. There is danger of heart trouble as a complication.

The patient should be kept very quiet and stay in bed as much as possible. The twitching ceases during sleep. The disease is likely to run several months. Drug treatment is not to be relied upon for cure, although there is a good deal of benefit from tonics to improve the blood. Arsenic and iron are prescribed.

## STYE

An inflammation of the fatty tissue of the eyelid close to its border, due to some constitutional condition. The treatment should be hot applications, to hasten the formation of pus, and incision as soon as it comes to a head. Sties are likely to appear in crops, and in such cases internal treatment should be prescribed by a physician.

## TONSILITIS

Tonsilitis is an inflammation of the tonsils, one or both tonsils becoming swollen and sensitive. There is some fever, and pains in the back and head. The cause is an infection and the disease is more or less contagious. The germs probably enter by way of the mouth. There is a simple or catarrhal form of tonsilitis, in which the inflammation usually lasts only a day or two. In a more severe form white spots appear upon the tonsils, caused by an exudation from them and the presence of bacteria. There is high fever, a feeling of weakness and loss of appetite. The more severe forms of tonsilitis may lead to the development of abscesses, which are known as quincy sores. Such abscesses should be opened, otherwise there is danger of blood poisoning. Recovery is slow, because of the weakness produced by the disease.

The treatment for tonsilitis should consist of the prompt administration of a cathartic, gargling or spraying the throat with some alkaline antiseptic, dioxygen being especially good for this purpose. Cold applications should be placed around the throat. Solid foods should be avoided.

## TOOTHACHE

Most of the troubles with teeth are due to decay, which is caused by certain bacteria that produce acids having the effect of dissolving the mineral substances which give the teeth their hardness. Holes in the teeth expose the inner sensitive pulp; inflammation follows, and there is intense pain. The inflammation is due to bacteria that may extend the trouble to the formation of an abscess beneath the cavity of the tooth.

Any trouble with the teeth requires the immediate attention of a dentist. It is important that the teeth should be kept clean and that frequent antiseptic preparations should be used to destroy the bacteria that make trouble in the teeth. As soon as a cavity is discovered, it should be scraped free of the diseased matter and filled with enamel, cement, gold or amalgam.

There are many preparations used to relieve toothache; none of them can be relied upon to stop it altogether so long as the tooth is in a diseased condition. Toothache may sometimes be relieved by filling the cavity with a little antiseptic cotton which has been saturated with oil of cloves, essence of peppermint, creosote, chloroform or menthol. Sometimes it may be relieved by painting the gum next to the tooth with iodine.

An abscess should be opened immediately by a dentist or physician. The old idea that an ulcerated tooth must not be extracted is a mistaken one. The sooner such a tooth is removed the better.

## TRICHINIASIS

A disease caused by a wormlike parasite called trichina. It enters the system through eating raw or partially cooked pork which contains the spores of the parasite. The spore is inclosed in a covering that opens in the stomach, and when it is free it passes into the intestines, where it grows to full size, and from the female parasite trichinæ multiply very rapidly. They make their way through the wall of the intestine and enter the tissues of the body. They lodge in the muscles and coil up in spiral form, where they become incrusted with a lime formation. They lodge chiefly in the muscles of the neck and upper part of the body.

A few days after eating infected pork one suffers from internal disturbances, including nausea, pains and usually diarrhea. Later, constipation sets in. As the parasites pass through the walls of the intestine and into the muscles pains increase, then stiffness of the muscles, soreness, eruptions of the skin and insomnia. Trichinæ often cause death.

There is little that can be done of a curative

nature, after the parasites have made their way into the muscles. Before they leave the intestine it is sometimes possible to prevent further trouble by the use of purges and vermifuges. Cooking meat kills trichinæ, and it is never safe to eat pork unless it has been cooked. Raw pork, either fresh or smoked, is liable to be infected and dangerous.

## TUMOR

An unnatural growth or enlargement of an organ or part of the body through the formation of new tissues which are of no use to the system. There are two general kinds of tumors, known as benign and malignant. The benign tumor usually grows slowly, separating the tissues around it as it increases in size. It is surrounded by distinct connective tissues, so that it is within a capsule, usually, and may be taken out of this with no disturbance to the surrounding tissue except at the place of incision, and such a tumor will not return.

Some of the less serious benign tumors appear upon the skin, such as warts, and are successfully treated with caustics.

The seriousness of the tumor depends not only upon its kind, but upon its location. For instance, many benign tumors are so located that they are inconvenient simply because of their size and weight, while others may be located either within or close to vital internal organs and thus cause pain and be very dangerous. A passage of the body may be closed by the formation of a tumor.

### Destructive Growths

Malignant tumors grow more rapidly than benign tumors and penetrate the substance of the surrounding tissues, displacing the healthy cells with destructive tissue, thus destroying muscle, fat, blood vessels, nerves, bones and skin, which are replaced by the tumor tissue. There is a great increase in the supply of blood, drawn by the rapid growth of the tumor. The spread of the disease may lead to decomposition, and there is danger of infection and ulceration. The more destructive tumors are called cancers.

In all cases the removal of malignant tumors is liable to be followed by a return of the disease. The ulcerated surface of a tumor is always liable to absorb bacterial poison and serious bleeding may also result. Tissues of an organ may be destroyed by the tumor tissue so as to cause death. But more often death results simply from exhaustion due to the progress of the disease.

When any lump or enlargement appears it should be regarded with suspicion and a physician or surgeon should be seen as soon as possible. A tumor may be removed when small with comparatively little danger, while later the operation would be difficult and dangerous. The danger of a return of the trouble is less when the removal occurs in the early stages, than after considerable development of the tumor. In all cases of malignant tumors their removal is liable to be followed by a return of the disease. There is no known remedy for tumors of the malignant type recognized by the medical profession except removal of the growth.

## TYPHOID FEVER

A disease of the intestines caused by germs that usually enter the body in water or milk. The germs infect the glands in the lower part of the small intestine, causing inflammation and swelling, followed by ulceration, sometimes hemorrhage, and occasionally perforation of the bowel. Toxins are produced by growth of the germs, causing high fever, prostration, and general poisoning.

The first symptoms of typhoid fever are a general feeling of illness, loss of appetite, severe headache and fever, gradually growing higher each day, for the first week. The temperature is lowest in the morning and gradually rises until night, remains practically stationary during the night, and the next morning gradually begins rising again. There is sometimes nose bleed among the early symptoms. Delicate rose-colored spots about the size of a pinhead appear upon the chest and abdomen, at about the end of the first week. There is tenderness and distention of the abdomen and diarrhea. There may be periods of delirium. The fever runs high and usually for about three weeks, when it begins to decrease gradually, disappearing at the end of another week, as a rule.

### Nursing of First Importance

The treatment should include first of all careful nursing, which is the most important thing throughout the period of illness. There should be frequent bathing to reduce the fever. Large quantities of water should be given to drink. There should be a carefully selected diet, avoiding milk. The weakened condition of the heart and all the muscles makes it especially necessary that the patient remain very quiet during the period of convalescence, and great care should be taken in the matter of diet.

## TYPHUS FEVER

A disease that is usually found only among persons who live under insanitary conditions, but the exact cause of it is not yet known. The first symptoms are headache, pains in the limbs, lassitude, followed by chills and fever, and vomiting. Then there are severe headaches and often stupor or delirium. One of the manifestations of the disease is rash, resembling that of typhoid, but more extensive and darker, which spreads over the entire body, beginning the second or third day. The spots are the result of bleeding under the skin.

During the second week the fever usually declines and the rash fades and recovery begins. Recovery follows in the majority of cases, but sometimes brain trouble and the effects of the high fever prove fatal.

The treatment should be similar to that for typhoid fever, and should be directed with especial reference to heart stimulation.

## VARICOSE VEINS

Varicose veins appear as enlargement of the superficial veins, usually of the leg. They occur most often in persons who have to stand a great deal, or after long walks, like forced marches of an army, and may develop during pregnancy. The veins increase in length as well as diameter, and appear in twisted cordlike masses, sometimes nearly the entire length of the leg. There is a feeling of fullness or pain in the leg, and sometimes severe cramp in the muscles. Congestion results in an unhealthy condition of the skin, which breaks down into ulcers that require special treatment to heal.

Treatment for varicose veins consists in rest and efforts to improve the circulation and reduce the size of the dilated veins, and an elastic stocking made to fit the limb is sometimes worn during the day and removed at night. In bad cases an operation to remove the dilated vein may be necessary.

## WHOOPING COUGH

This disease is contagious and epidemic in childhood, and manifests itself by a spasmodic cough, ending with the characteristic long-drawn inspiration called the whoop. The first symptom usually is that of a common cold in the head, with a chronic cough. The peculiar cough of the disease then develops. There are intervals when the child is apparently well, but the coughing spells occur frequently. The child becomes red in the face and almost strangles, and the coughing frequently ends in vomiting.

The disease runs about two months usually, and then gradually passes away. Children under a year old are especially in danger of complications from bronchitis, leading to broncho-pneumonia.

The treatment should include a simple diet, fresh air night and day, avoiding conditions that might cause taking cold, and special treatment should be given under the direction of a physician.

## WORMS

Intestinal parasites or worms are frequent causes of disturbing conditions in children. The symptoms are derangement of the digestive organs, nervousness, restlessness at night and grinding of the teeth in sleep, picking of the nose, and rolling of the head.

Round worms, which are about three inches long, are sometimes discharged by administering drugs which may be safely used by a physician. Thread worms or pin worms are attached to the lower part of the large intestine. Symptoms of their presence include itching sensations in that region. They are best removed by injecting eight ounces of an infusion of quassia, each morning, having it retained half an hour.

One of the most troublesome of the intestinal parasites is the tapeworm, which is very long. It is usual for only a few segments of the worm to be discharged at one time, leaving the head attached to the mucous membrane of the intestine. So long as this remains new segments form, and the tapeworm lives on.

In order to discharge the head, the patient is made to fast for 12 hours, overnight, and in the morning a preparation of pomegranate root in sweetened water is administered. An hour or two later a cathartic should be given, which will discharge the tapeworm, including the head.

## WENS

A small, ball-like formation of fat under the scalp caused by some obstruction of the outlets of the surface of glands in the skin. They are usually quite small, but sometimes are large enough to be unsightly. There is danger of their becoming infected and developing inflammation. They should be removed by surgical operation, which is simple, because the wen lies just beneath the skin.

## YELLOW FEVER

A disease of warm climates. It is caused by a germ spread by a certain kind of mosquito. The first symptom is a chill, followed by moderate fever. The pulse is weak and usually not over 100 a minute. Nausea and vomiting are persistent, especially in fatal cases. Hemorrhages occur from various organs, including the stomach and bowels.

The treatment is first mild laxatives, followed by light stimulants and quinine. Cleanliness and quiet are essential. The patient's bed should be screened from mosquitos to prevent them from carrying the disease to other individuals.

The preventive measures employed include cleanliness and thorough drainage, pouring kerosene oil upon stagnant water in the neighborhood, and thoroughly screening to keep out mosquitos.

## PERIODS OF INFECTION

Table showing the number of days that may elapse between exposure to an infectious disease and the time when the first symptoms of the disease appear—called the period of incubation; the number of days that the disease is likely to run; and the number of days during which there is danger of communicating the disease to another person. The sign + means that the period of infection may extend beyond the time indicated, because certain conditions attending the disease persist.

|  | Incubation period | Period of illness | Infective period |
|---|---|---|---|
| Chicken pox ....... | 10 to 16 | 3 to 7 | 21 to 28 |
| Diphtheria ......... | 2 to 12 | 10 to 14 | 21 to 28+ |
| Erysipelas ........ | 1 to 8 | 4 to 6 | 12 to 16 |
| German measles ... | 7 to 21 | 3 to 7 | 21 |
| Grippe ........... | 1 to 7 | 3 to 14 | 3 to 14 |
| Infantile paralysis .. | 4 to 28 | 10 to 28 | 28 |
| Measles .......... | 10 to 14 | 7 to 8 | 21+ |
| Mumps ........... | 10 to 22 | 3 to 7 | 21 to 28+ |
| Scarlet fever ...... | 1 to 10 | 7 to 14 | 42+ |
| Smallpox ......... | 7 to 16 | 12 to 16 | 28 to 56+ |
| Typhoid fever ..... | 7 to 21 | 14 to 28 | 14 to 28+ |
| Whooping cough .. | 7 to 14 | 42 to 56 | 35 to 56+ |

# MORE ABOUT HYGIENE

## CONSUMPTION CURED WHILE WORKING

Probably no disease has received so much attention during the last quarter century as consumption, and, fortunately, the results have been very encouraging. Tuberculosis is no longer regarded as the hopelessly fatal malady that it seemed to be years ago, the death rate having decreased one-half during the past generation. The reason for it does not lie in any newly discovered medicine or in any method of administering medicines new or old. There is probably hardly a person living in the United States who has not many times had within his body the germs of tuberculosis. The reason that we do not all die of the disease is that elements within the body and the elements of nature combine to destroy the germs of the disease and to fortify the organs and the tissues of the body against their attacks. Three important things are involved in the cure of consumption. The first is pure outdoor air; the second is rest; and the third ample nourishment.

Long ago it was discovered that persons going from one locality to another sometimes recovered from consumption if the change was made during the early stages of the disease. In such cases the change was usually from bad air and close quarters to good air and plenty of it out of doors. But against the record of such cures has been a long, sad record of disappointment and death far from home and among unpleasant surroundings. For

A Friend Worth While

Make friends with the colts and other healthful and active, domestic animals. Their healthfulness and natural play spirit is contagious. Many have found better health with a good horse on the farm.

### Like the Way of Health

The highway of health leads always straight away. It lies under clear skies in the bright sunshine and fresh air. On either hand verdant grass and trees, and all of life-filled and life-giving nature add their impulse and their sustaining vitality. The way may be rough, and often is up steep places, but it is always straight ahead.

instance, many have heard that consumption could be cured by going into the deserts of Arizona. Many a man has gone there, sent by unwise relatives and advisers, to seek health by roughing it. Without sufficient money or strength to successfully meet conditions, the unfortunate victim has suffered from homesickness, exposure and lack of proper nourishment, with fatal results. Many cures have been accomplished in sanitariums, which are often at a considerable distance from the home of the consumptive. It may be quite expensive to go to such an institution, and this expense may be beyond one's resources. Then, too, the consumptive may be the mainstay of a dependent family, and to leave home seems to be out of the question.

## Home Cure for Workers

It is to meet such conditions that extensive experiments have been undertaken by tuberculosis experts. The results have been remarkably successful. The purpose is to treat patients while they are at home and continue their regular work. It is, of course, important to begin the treatment just as soon as symptoms of tuberculosis can be discovered, if possible. There should always be a sharp lookout for symptoms of the disease, and, if suspected, a good doctor can find out whether or not tuberculosis is present by the very simple blood test which is now used. The treatment is vigorous, but the results are so gratifying and positive that it should be attractive rather than otherwise.

## Sleep in Open Air

First of all, the tuberculosis doctor insists that the consumptive must sleep in the open air. If it is not feasible to provide an open porch upon which to sleep, the alternative is to remove the windows of the sleeping room during the night. Of course, protection from storm must be provided, but it is essential that there should be full and free circulation of the outer air for the patient to breathe.

## Overheated Living Rooms

Another reform in the daily habits is that of lowering the temperature of houses and places of business. It is said that most people maintain a tropical jungle atmosphere in their houses. This is very harmful, and has its effect in the prevalence of disease. The intense heat takes the moisture out of the air, and it then becomes irritating to the mucous membranes and enervating to the whole system. The temperature of living rooms should not be above 65 degrees, and not only should higher temperature be avoided, but special care should be given to the matter of ventilation in order that the air may be pure.

## Daily Cold Bath

Some of the best doctors lay much stress upon the daily cold bath. In the incipient cases of consumption experience seems to prove that it is highly beneficial. Sluggishness of circulation through the skin accompanies tuberculosis. General elimination becomes imperfect. The stimulus and cleanliness of the daily bath count toward recovery.

For some persons the cold bath, if taken without milder baths leading up to it, during a reasonable period of time, may be positively dangerous, but this is not true of most persons. A cold bath quickly taken, followed by a brisk rub, is invigorating, and not only tones up the surface of the body but helps to tone up the entire system. All of this is in the line of hardening and making the body, its tissues and organs, more vigorous. The greater the success attained in this direction the more completely is the body fortified against disease, and the more completely are the bacteria of disease repelled.

## Abundant Nourishment

The successful treatment of incipient consumption requires an abundance of nourishing food. The digestive organs should not be loaded down with rich foods, highly seasoned and difficult to digest, otherwise digestion will be impaired. The food should be plain and easily digested, including coarse breads and cereals in various forms, mature meats not overcooked, all the good milk that one can drink and plenty of good vegetables and fruit.

Outdoor exercise and deep breathing should be made a daily habit, and clothes enough for comfort, but no more than is really necessary for protection, should be worn. Care should be taken to avoid chilling and taking cold.

If one is able to work, he can follow this treatment without in the least interfering with his regular everyday duties. Many have done so, and without losing time from their work or being to the expense that would be involved in the same treatment at a sanitarium, have been cured of consumption permanently.

## Limitations

It must not be understood that everyone suffering from tuberculosis, even in the comparatively early stages, will be able to work all day under insanitary conditions and recover, although following these directions. It is always best to put one's self into the hands of a competent physician, who should be able to judge whether the victim can continue his daily duties or must give up work for a time.

## GENERAL BOOTH'S LONGEVITY RECIPE

The aged founder and commander-in-chief of the Salvation Army says:

Eat as little as possible. The average man eats too much. Instead of nourishing the body, he overtaxes it, compelling his stomach to digest more food than it has capacity for.

Drink plenty of water in preference to adulterated concoctions. Water is wholesome nourishment.

Take exercise. It is just as foolish to develop the mind and not the body as it is to develop the body and not the mind. Perform some manual labor; dig, walk, chop wood, or, if you can talk with your whole body, why then talk; but do it with all your might.

Have a system, but do not be a slave of the system. If my hour to rise is 8 A. M., and at that time I haven't had sufficient rest I take a longer time.

Do not fill your life with a lot of silly and sordid pleasures, so that when you come to die you will find you have not really lived.

Abstain from indulgences which overtax the body and injure not only yourself, but the generations that come after you.

Have a purpose in life that predominates above all else, that is beneficent to those about you, and not to your own greedy self alone. If there is one thing for which I am glad, it is that I have found a purpose which involves not me alone, but all humanity.

## HORACE FLETCHER'S RULES FOR EATING

1. Eat only in response to an actual appetite which will be satisfied with plain bread and butter.

2. Chew all the solid food until it is liquid and practically swallows itself.

3. Sip and taste all liquids that have taste, such as soup and lemonade. Water has no taste and can be swallowed immediately.

4. Never taste food while angry or worried, and only when calm. Waiting for the mood in connection with the appetite is a speedy cure for both anger and worry.

Remember and practice these four rules and your teeth and health will be fine.

## HEART FAILURE FROM OVEREATING

The heart is about as perfect an organ as any in the body, and one that rarely shirks its duty. It commences its labors during early infancy, and goes on until the last moment of life, without intermission for 75 years or more. At every beat it propels two ounces of blood through its structure. At 75 pulsations a minute, nine pounds of blood are sucked in and pumped out. Every hour, 540 pounds; every day 12,960 pounds; every year 4,730,-400 pounds; every 100 years 473,040,000 pounds.

Now, the heart has for a neighbor an organ, the stomach, very fond of self-indulgence. The stomach lies directly under the heart with only the diaphragm between, and when it fills with gas it is like a small balloon, and lifts up until it interferes directly with the heart's action. The stomach never generates gas, but when filled with undigested food fermentation takes place and gas is formed. The interference depends upon the amount of gas in the stomach.

To overcome this obstruction, the heart has to exert itself in proportion to the interference, more blood is sent to the brain, and the following symptoms are the result: A dizzy head, a flushed face, loss of sight, spots or blurs before the eyes, flashes of light, zigzag lines or chains, etc., often followed by severe headache. These symptoms are usually relieved when the gas is expelled from the stomach.

Now, when this upward pressure upon the heart becomes excessive, more dangerous symptoms supervene, a large quantity of blood is sent to the brain, some vessel ruptures, and a blood clot in the brain is the result, and the person dies of apoplexy, or, if he lives, is a cripple for life. When a sick person, or an old one, or one with feeble digestion sleeps, digestion is nearly or quite suspended, but fermentation goes on, and gas is generated as before stated. A man is found dead in bed and the physician says he had heart failure. The heart failed from overloading just as a horse might do.

Again, a man is sick with typhoid fever or pneumonia, or almost any other disease, and dies of heart failure; but what has his diet been during the sickness? At present it is very fashionable to commence with what might well be called the stuffing process. Iced milk, which is so cool and grateful to the patient, from three pints to one gallon during the day and night. How unwise!

Moral: If you don't want to have your heart fail don't abuse it, don't overload it.—[*Journal of Hygiene*.

# The Conservation of Human Life

THE movement in behalf of the conservation of the natural resources of the country has naturally led to consideration of the greater problem of national efficiency. This depends, not only on physical environment, but on social environment, and most of all on human vitality. The government has had special investigation made along this line, and through the National Conservation Commission, Prof. Irving Fisher of Yale University, a member of the commission, has made an important report on National Vitality: Its Wastes and Conservation. We quote from the report:

## CONSERVATION THROUGH HYGIENE

Personal hygiene is not only of direct importance to the individual, but furnishes the public opinion from which, and from which alone, sound public and semi-public hygiene can spring. Public hygiene will be ineffective unless supported by personal hygiene. The milk and water supply of a city may be ideal as supplied at a dwelling, but may be carelessly contaminated there. Observation shows that many of the world's most vital men and women have practiced hygiene and often thereby turned weak constitutions into strong ones.

Personal hygiene comprises hygiene of environment (air, soil, dwellings, clothing), hygiene of nutrition, and hygiene of activity. The ideal conditions of health require purity in air, purity and proper use of food, and a proper balance between mental and physical activity, rest and sleep. The present world-wide interest in personal hygiene and physical education is not due to any startling discoveries, but to rediscovery of importance of truths long insisted upon by the medical profession.

## The Hygiene of Environment

The prime factor in environment is the atmosphere. Originally man was doubtless an outdoor animal. Civilization has brought him an indoor environment, and with it tuberculosis. Experiments in hospitals have shown that the agitation of the air by dry sweeping greatly increases bacteria. Air in a confined room may be contaminated by chemicals in wallpaper, plaster or mortar.

The one place in which the individual has the most control over his air supply is the bedroom. The fashion now of sleeping with wide-open windows, or even out-of-doors, is certain to improve American vitality. The windows of living and work rooms also may be open even in winter if a window board is used to deflect the air upward and prevent a cold stratum forming on the floor. The outdoor life or the abundant use of fresh air is an almost certain preventive of colds.

This fact was commented upon by Franklin over a century ago, and has been rediscovered many times since, especially in the experience of army troops. The evils of bad air are not confined to its chemical content. A room is sometimes "close" simply because it is hot or overmoist or devoid of any air current.

The effect of air on the skin and of radiation of heat from the body is important. Consequently, a proper use of air involves a proper use of clothing, which needs to be both porous and light.

Closely connected with air hygiene is the hygiene of light. "Where sun and air enter seldom the physician enters often." The lighting of dwellings and schoolrooms is especially important with reference to the eyes. This is true also of even the color and texture of the printed page we read. Probably one-fourth of all educated people in America suffer from disturbances due more or less to eye strain and its numerous indirect effects.

## The Hygiene of Nutrition

The scientific study of diet has only just begun, and few authoritative results can yet be stated. That diet has a distinct relation to endurance has been rendered probable by many investigations, which seem to show in particular that avoidance of overeating, and especially an excess in protein, and thorough mastication are wholesome rules. In the choice of foods the individual must be given a wide latitude. His own instinct, restored and educated by avoiding food bolting, which blunts it, will probably be a truer guide than the wisest of physiologists. Diseased foods, such as oysters polluted with sewage, may transmit typhoid and other maladies.

## Drug Habits

Poisons, whether taken into the body or produced within, are injurious. The commonest form of intoxication is alcoholic. Its evils are becoming more apparent than ever before. As Metchnikoff says, it lowers the resistance of the white corpuscles, which are the natural defenders of the body. It predisposes to tuberculosis, and numerous other diseases.

The evils of tobacco are less, and are less appreciated. Its stunting effects on the growing child are especially harmful.

## Activity Hygiene

It is an encouraging sign of the times that baths are coming more into vogue, both through the private bathtub for the wealthy and the public baths for the poor. During the last generation the importance of exercise has come to be acknowledged, due largely to the growth of modern athletics. The athletic ideal of the Greeks was, however, higher than that which now prevails in this country. Over-exertion, physical and mental, is one of the chief American faults. The danger signal of fatigue is seldom observed, and the instinct for recreation and amusement is often stifled.

## Sex Hygiene

Undue reticence on this subject is responsible for the general ignorance as to the extent to which the abuse of the sex relation is injuring this and every nation, physically, mentally, and morally. Syphilis poisons the blood and affects all parts of the body. It makes the individual a " bad risk " for life insurance companies for several years, and is likely to be transmitted to others through a kiss or through the use of a common towel, while the danger of transmitting from husband to wife, or vice versa, continues for many years. Syphilis is one of the few really hereditary diseases, and the saddest of all facts connected with it is that the guilty parent may escape and the innocent children suffer.

Gonorrhea, while usually cured without apparent impairment of health, destroys fertility, and for years after it has apparently ceased may be re-aroused. It is responsible for a large number of the cases of infantile blindness and for a larger percentage of many of the serious troubles of women. The social diseases, while seldom assigned as a cause of death, are known to predispose to other diseases and greatly to shorten life.

## THINGS WHICH NEED TO BE DONE

1. The National Government, the States, and the municipalities should steadfastly devote their energies and resources to the protection of the people from disease. Such protection is quite as properly a governmental function as is protection from foreign invasion, from criminals or from fire. It is both bad policy and bad economy to leave this work mainly to the weak and spasmodic efforts of charity, or to the philanthropy of physicians.

The national government should exercise at least three public health functions: First, investigation; second, the dissemination of information; third, administration.

It should remove the reproach that more pains are now taken to protect the health of farm cattle than of human beings. It should provide more and greater laboratories for research in preventive medicine and public hygiene. Provision should also be made for better and more universal vital statistics, without which it is impossible to know the exact conditions in an epidemic, or in general, the sanitary or insanitary conditions in any part of the country. It should aim, as should state and municipal legislation, to procure adequate registration of births, statistics of which are at present lacking throughout the United States.

The National government should prevent transportation of disease from State to State in the same way as it now provides for foreign quarantine and the protection of the nation from the importation of diseases of foreign immigrants. It should provide for the protection of the passenger in interstate railway travel from infection by his fellow-passengers and from insanitary conditions in sleeping cars, etc.

It should enact suitable legislation providing against pollution of interstate streams.

## Health Education

It should provide for the dissemination of information in regard to the prevention of tuberculosis and other diseases, the dangers of impure air, impure foods, impure milk, imperfect sanitation, ventilation, etc. Just as now the Department of Agriculture supplies specific information to the farmer in respect to raising crops or live stock, so should one of the departments, devoted principally to health and education, be able to provide every health officer, school teacher, employer, physician and private family with specific information in regard to public, domestic and personal hygiene.

It should provide for making the national capital into a model sanitary city, free from sanitary tenements and workshops, air pollution, food pollution, water pollution, etc., with a rate of death and a rate of illness among infants, and among the population generally, so low and so free from epidemics of typhoid or other diseases as will arouse the attention of the entire country and the world.

There should be a constant adaptation of the pure-food laws to changing conditions. Meat inspection and other inspection should be so arranged as to protect not only foreigners, but our own citizens. The existing health agencies of the government should be concentrated in one department, better co-ordinated and given more powers and appropriations.

## State Regulation

3. State boards of health and state legislation should provide for the regulation of labor of women, should make physiological conditions for women's work and prevent their employment before and after childbirth; should regulate the age at which children shall be employed, make reasonable regulations in regard to hours of labor and against the dangers in hazardous trades, and especially against the particular dangers of dust and poisonous chemicals; should make regulations for sanitation and provide inspection of factories, schools, asylums, prisons and other public institutions.

Where municipalities have not the powers to enact the legislation above mentioned with reference to local conditions, the necessary legislation or authority should be provided by the State. Or where by reason of the small size of the town no efficient local action is possible, the State should exercise the necessary functions. It should in such cases advise and supervise local boards of health. It should have an engineering department and advise regarding the construction of sewers and water supplies. Pollution of such supplies, unless entirely local, should be prevented by the State, which should be equipped with laboratories for the analysis of water, milk and other foods.

Suitable legislation should be passed regulating the sale of drugs, especially preparations containing cocaine, opium or alcohol. Legislation, not too far in advance of public sentiment needed to enforce it, should be passed regulating the sale of alcoholic beverages. State registration of births, deaths and cases of illness should be much more general and efficient than at present.

## Local Health Board Duties

4. Municipal boards of health need to have more powers and greater appropriations; less political interference and better trained health officers; more support in public opinion. Their ordinances in regard to expectoration, notification of infectious disease, etc., should be better enforced.

More legislation should be advocated, passed and enforced to the end that streets may be kept clean, garbage properly removed, sewage properly disposed of, air pollution of all kinds prevented, whether by smoke, street dust, noxious gases or any other source. Noises should also be lessened.

Municipalities need also to take measures to prevent infection being carried by flies, mosquitoes, other insects and vermin, and by prostitution. They need to guard with great care the water supply, and in many cases to filter it; they should make standards for milk purity and enforce them; they should also regularly inspect other foods exposed for sale; provide for sanitary inspection of local slaughterhouses, dairies, shops, lodging and boarding houses, and other establishments within the power of the particular municipality; they should make and enforce stricter building laws, especially as relating to tenements, to the end that dark-room tenements may be eliminated and all tenements be provided with certain minimum standard requirements as to light, air and sanitation.

## In the Schools

5. School children should be medically inspected and school hygiene universally practiced. This in-

volves better protection against school epidemics, better ventilation, light and cleanliness of the schoolroom, the discovery and correction of adenoids, eye strain, and nervous strain generally, and the provision for playgrounds. Sound scientific hygiene should be taught in all schools.

6. The curricula of medical schools should be rearranged with a greater emphasis on prevention and on the training of health officers. Sanatoria and hospitals, dispensaries, district nursing, tuberculosis classes and other semi-public institutions should be increased in number and improved in quality. The medical profession, keeping pace with these changes, should be the chief means of conveying their benefits to the public. Universities and research institutions need to take up the study of hygiene in all its branches. Now that the diseases of childhood are receiving attention, the next step should be to study the diseases of middle life. These are diseases, to a large extent, of nutrition and circulation.

## Corporations May Help

7. In industrial and commercial establishments employers may greatly aid the health movement, and in many cases make their philanthropy self-supporting by providing social secretaries, lunch and rest rooms, physiological (generally shorter) hours of work, provision for innocent amusements, seats for women, etc.

Life insurance companies could properly and with much profit club together to instruct their risks in self-care and secure general legislation and enforcement of legislation in behalf of public health.

## Change in Habits of Living

8. The present striking change in personal habits of living should be carried out to its logical conclusion until the health ideals and the ideals of athletic training shall become universal. This change involves a quiet revolution in habits of living, a more intelligent utilization of one's environment, especially in regard to the condition of the air in our houses, the character of the clothes we wear, of the site and architecture of the dwelling with respect to sunlight, soil, ventilation and sanitation, the character of food, its cooking, the use of alcohol, tobacco and drugs, and last, but not least, sex hygiene in all its bearings.

9. The fight against disease will aid in the fight against pauperism and crime. It is also true that any measures which tend to eliminate poverty, vice, and crime will tend to improve sanitary conditions.

## Marriage of the Fit

10. Finally, eugenics, or hygiene for future generations, should be studied and gradually put in practice. This involves the prohibition of flagrant cases of marriages of the unfit, such as syphilitics, the insane, feeble-minded, epileptics, paupers or criminals, etc. The example of Indiana in this regard should be considered and followed by other States, as also in regard to the unsexing of rapists, criminals, idiots and degenerates generally.

A public opinion should be aroused which will not only encourage healthy and discountenance degenerate marriages, but will become so embedded in the minds of the rising generation as to unconsciously, but powerfully, affect marriage choices.

# INDEX

# 252    INDEX